FOUL DEEDS & SUSPICIOUS DEATHS
AROUND CAMBRIDGE

Foul Deeds and Suspicious Deaths Around

CAMBRIDGE

Glenda Goulden

Wharncliffe Books

First published in Great Britain in 2007 by
Wharncliffe Books
an imprint of
Pen & Sword Books Ltd
47 Church Street
Barnsley
South Yorkshire
S70 2AS

ISBN: 978 184560 10 2

A CIP catalogue record for this book is available from
the British Library

Typeset in Plantin and ITC Benguiat by
Mousemat Design Limited

Printed and bound in Great Britain by CPI UK

Pen & Sword Books Ltd incorporates the Imprints of
Pen & Sword Aviation, Pen & Sword Maritime,
Pen & Sword Military, Wharncliffe Local History,
Pen and Sword Select, Pen and Sword Military Classics
and Leo Cooper.

For a complete list of Pen & Sword titles please contact
PEN & SWORD BOOKS LIMITED
47 Church Street, Barnsley, South Yorkshire,
S70 2AS, England
E-mail: enquiries@pen-and-sword.co.uk
Website: www.pen-and-sword.co.uk

Contents

Acknowledgements

Many people have helped me in various ways in the compilation of this book and I am grateful to them all. I would like, especially, to acknowledge the invaluable contribution made by Chris Jakes and the staff of the Cambridgeshire Collection at Cambridge Central Library, and Rupert Harding of Pen and Sword Books Ltd.

Introduction

In the second half of the twentieth century Cambridge was a city, but a small one. It was more like a large market town with a university in the middle of it, one of the most renowned universities in the world. It was famous for the splendour of its colleges and for the beauty of the River Cam flowing along the Backs and on into the flat, fertile Cambridgeshire fens.

Towards the end of the century it could be considered that the most serious problems faced by those living, working or studying in Cambridge were the traffic, which at times brought the narrow streets in its centre to a standstill, and the high price of even the most modest property, forcing many to make their homes in rented flats or bedsits or to commute.

Beyond Cambridge, the area was mainly agricultural, with rich acres – a vibrant mix of greens and golds throughout the summer months. Wheat, barley, potatoes and sugar beet were grown in abundance, with gradually more acid-yellow flowered oilseed rape being grown. Twelve or so miles to the east a living crop was grown – the thoroughbred racehorse. Around Newmarket the paddocks of the studs were lush green, neatly fenced and hedged, and the heath, with its two racecourses, was the largest stretch of tended grassland in the world.

The area was not heavily populated. It had few towns of any size. But it did have smaller market towns and numerous villages, such as Thriplow, Arrington and Grantchester, many of them with a wealthy country house or estate close by.

Rural though it was, the Cambridge area had good roads linking it to, within easy reach, Royston, Huntingdon, Bedford, Peterborough and Ely, and further afield with London, the Midlands and the east coast ports of Felixstowe and Harwich.

It could be thought that it was without many of the worst disadvantages associated with life in the more populated urban areas of the country. That it was an attractive place to be. But timeworn walls and green fields were no guarantee. Nowhere was without crime, its perpetrators and its victims.

From the 1950s, through towards the end of the century, over the years remembered here, the area suffered the whole gamut of crime and disorder, from violent death to violence on the streets, rape to robbery and riot, some of the more serious offences making national headlines.

Throughout those years the area was effectively policed, as well as could be expected for most of them. But, at times, the 'thin blue line' became very thin. The 1970s in particular were years when a shortage of manpower coincided with a steep rise in offences of all kinds and the streets of Cambridge and Cambridgeshire became some of the most dangerous in the country.

In 1974, a newly-created Cambridgeshire Constabulary had to deal with a thirty-six per cent rise in crime, one of the largest rises of any police force in England. It had one of the highest crime rates per head of the population outside of London. In 1975, 854 crimes of violence were reported to police. They included murder, attempted murder, the threat of murder, manslaughter, felonious wounding, malicious wounding and assault. Sexual assaults also figured. Taking differences in population numbers into consideration, there was a three times greater chance of a person becoming a victim of crime in Cambridge than in hard-hitting Glasgow.

No one could explain that. Cambridgeshire police had an eighty-seven per cent clear-up rate on cases of violence, and of 301 reported cases in Cambridge itself in 1975 all but forty-four were brought to court.

What the escalation in crime did show was that such a high certainty of being arrested was not acting as a deterrent, particularly obvious in the constant hooliganism of supporters of Cambridge United following the club's promotion to the Football League in 1970. It was felt that the magistrates' courts were partly to blame in such cases for not backing up the police by imposing maximum sentences on offenders.

And that also applied to the 151 cases of assault on Cambridgeshire police officers in 1975. Only seven assailants were sent to prison, half were fined between £3 and £50, and only one was fined the maximum of £100. The average fine was £30 for hitting an officer on duty and £8 for resisting arrest. The most usual fine was a mere £5, despite Inspector Geoffrey Chandler of the Cambridgeshire Police Federation saying: 'I am extremely concerned at the swing towards violence against police officers. Police officers are being assaulted more often and I would like to see severe attacks met with severe sentences from the courts.' His feelings were echoed by the Cambridgeshire Chief Constable, Mr Frederick Drayton Porter.

Matters had not improved a year later. In August 1976, the Home Office declared Cambridgeshire to be one of the five top provincial forces dealing with the highest crime rates, higher than Lancashire and Yorkshire, the Home Counties and the Thames Valley. Merseyside and Greater Manchester were worse but, when population levels were taken into account, Cambridge city topped them.

Yet, despite the Home Office being aware of the high Cambridgeshire crime rate, in December 1976 the Government ordered a sharp cutback in police spending. There had to be economies in various areas, one being the employment of civilian staff. The most far-reaching consequence was that the county's cadet force ceased to exist. The system of introducing teenagers to police work, each course being heavily over-subscribed, had served the force well for a number of years and a quarter of serving officers had come into the force from the cadets. It was a critical loss at a time of manpower shortages and difficulties in non-cadet recruitment. Of the enforced axing the Cambridgeshire Deputy Chief Constable, Mr Frank Ash, said: 'At a time when policemen have been needed more than ever and when the crime rate is still not dropping, it is criminal.'

The Home Secretary, Merlyn Rees, in July 1977, asked for a report on the police situation in Cambridgeshire, aware that law and order was under threat because of the county's crime rate, which remained high. Mr Victor Gilbert, a former Special Branch chief and the newly-appointed successor to Drayton Porter as Chief Constable, said that he would make a fresh study of the situation in the county and, through Her Majesty's Inspector of Constabulary, would report back to the Home Secretary.

It was felt that low police pay levels and an inadequate cash allocation were at the root of the problem. Without more money that 'thin blue line' would reach breaking point. Besides a shortage of officers on the streets and the roads, there was no money to pay detectives overtime and criminals were going free.

Francis Pym, the MP for Cambridgeshire, said: 'It is clear that there is a continuing concern and investigation into the county. I am sure it will be a relief to the people of Cambridgeshire that the Home Secretary will receive an up-to-date report from Her Majesty's Inspector.' Perhaps it would be. But would it help the day-to-day situation on the streets of Cambridge when the constabulary was pushed to even police Newmarket Road on Cambridge United match days?

A response by Gilbert was a plan to put more officers on patrol on the streets of Cambridgeshire by giving uniformed officers the chance to work on their eight rest days each month. That would, in effect, halve the force's deficit of seventy officers and the shortfall problem would be eased.

Charles Naan, the long-serving head of the Cambridgeshire CID and at that time Acting Assistant Chief Constable, said of the plan: 'The object is to get as many more policemen as possible out on patrol. The Chief Constable is intent on using every available method in order to deal with the general policing situation in Cambridgeshire.'

The shortfall of seventy, five per cent of the requirement for the county, reflected the ongoing recruitment difficulties. There were no cadets, and the area's young men and women were reluctant to put themselves forward to be hit in the face with a bottle or punched to the ground. Naan believed that the low starting salary was to blame. He said: 'As things are at the moment that salary is little more than those men would be getting on the dole.'

At the same time, August 1977, Judge David Wild who, at the end of 1976, had heard the longest and most complex criminal trial ever to be held in Cambridge and had jailed a local gang of thieves, said that because of the number of recent cases of unprovoked assault on innocent citizens he would hand out long deterrent jail sentences if violence on the streets of Cambridge did not stop. Within twenty-four hours of that statement, two gangs of youths battled in the recently-opened Lion Yard shopping complex in the city centre in the middle of the afternoon, endangering shoppers and forcing shopkeepers to close and lock their doors. One youth was arrested.

Drayton Porter left the police force at the end of June 1977 after a career of forty-four years, his retirement coming at one of the worst times for the local force. But, in July, the Cambridgeshire Constabulary was given the boost that Drayton Porter had lobbied for when county councillors, alarmed at sagging detection rates, agreed that law and order was the county's number one priority. There was to be more money in the 1978-79 budget to help police with their crime detection problems.

It was badly needed. In 1977, there was record crime, a serious shortage of officers, and detectives were taking on double the caseload recommended by the Home Office. Cambridgeshire crime figures, released in May 1978, showed that crimes of violence and robbery were down while everything else, burglary, shoplifting and theft, showed increases averaging out at over twenty-eight percent. Sex offences increased by fifty-five per cent.

In October 1977, Victor Gilbert said that the percentage increases in Cambridgeshire meant that about 3,300 more crimes per year were being committed. Recruiting problems apart, the pressure on existing officers, coupled with grievances about low pay, was bringing more resignations from the force. He said: 'Many policemen are voting with their feet and walking out of the force to take up better-paid jobs.' And safer. As he spoke, three Cambridgeshire officers were in hospital after 'violent incidents involving criminals'.

Despite those ongoing problems the Cambridgeshire force excelled itself in case after case, never more so than in the biggest criminal investigation in local policing history – the search for and arrest of the Cambridge Rapist, Peter Samuel Cook, in the mid-1970s. In the wake of that success the leader of the investigation, Detective Superintendent Bernard Hotson, the Deputy Commander of the county CID under Detective Chief Superintendent Charles Naan, became the Cambridge Divisional Commander and was promoted to the rank of Chief Superintendent. Just one example of the good leadership essential to the detection of the more serious crimes.

Professor Francis E Camps, the finest pathologist in the country in the 1950s and 1960s, who was brought into the area to help in solving the murders of Rachel Parsons in Newmarket and Cacilie Wollner in Cambridge, said that whatever the advances in science, medicine and technology, they were only a complement to careful, methodical and experienced police investigation. That remained so as forensics began to make more progress than Camps could ever have dreamed possible.

Camps was one of about twenty-four Home Office pathologists in the country. In Cambridgeshire that post was filled for thirty years from 1962 by Wrexham-born, former Cambridge medical student, Austin Gresham; lecturer and then Professor of Morbid Anatomy and Histopathology at the University of Cambridge, based at Addenbrooke's Hospital, who was called in to aid police in the investigation of murders or unexplained deaths. Known for his pipe, his bow ties and his waspish sense of humour, he once recalled nights spent at murder scenes with: 'It was usually bloody cold and on occasions you nearly drowned yourself. But it was interesting, sometimes fun.' Of the county's 900 to 1000 post-mortems carried out each year he said that, on average, only twenty were of murder or in need of criminal investigation while, in London, there was one murder a week and, at times, one a day. The Cambridge coroner for many of Gresham's years serving the county was Dudley Durell who felt he had been fortunate to have had him to rely on. His forensic work was meticulous. 'His solutions were conclusive and rarely questioned.' He retired in 1992, one of his last major inquiries having nothing to do with Cambridge or Cambridgeshire. He was called upon to examine the remains of Suffolk girl Julie Ward, determining that she had been murdered in the Masai Mara Game Reserve in Kenya and had not, as claimed, been eaten by wild animals.

Of the most vital importance in cases of murder was a good police officer in charge of an efficient team, with confidence in the forensic experts, psychologists and psychiatrists brought in to assist and a willingness to cooperate with other police forces. On the occasions when Scotland Yard's murder squad was called in to assist the local force there was only commendation. Of the 1960 search for killer Gypsy Jack Smith, John du Rose said: 'I found the Cambridgeshire force well trained and as efficient as any force in the country. They made endless inquiries and were tireless in their desire to find the killer.' As successfully, local police worked with the Metropolitan Police on the battering to death of Janice Weston on the A1 in 1983 and, in the following year, with Interpol and the police forces of three European countries as they masterminded the arrest of the gunman who had murdered a postmistress in the small Cambridgeshire village of Thriplow.

While police forces in Bedfordshire, Suffolk and other adjacent areas were involved in the solution of some of the crimes here they were, for the most part, dealt with by the Cambridgeshire force. That force changed, over the years, in name and area, a fact not always clear when published reports refer only to 'police in Cambridge' or 'Cambridgeshire police'. I am indebted to Bob Wordsworth, a long-serving officer with the Cambridgeshire Constabulary, for clarification of the city and county forces during the period covered here.

The present Cambridgeshire Constabulary was formed in

1974 after the reorganisation of county boundaries and the formation of the new Police Authority. It replaced the Mid-Anglia Constabulary which had been in existence since 1965, the creation of the man who was to become its first Chief Constable and go on to lead the Cambridgeshire Constabulary, Frederick Drayton Porter. He had formed the Mid-Anglia by bringing together a number of forces dating back to 1836 – the Cambridgeshire County Police, Huntingdonshire Constabulary, Isle of Ely Constabulary, Peterborough Combined Police and the Cambridge City Police. They all had a proud history of preserving law and order in their own areas which was carried forward to the new, and present, county force.

The seriousness of some of the crimes the local forces were called upon to deal with show that the Cambridge area was no more free of the minority in society drawn to do wrong, than the supposedly more lawless major conurbations. Over the years, for a variety of reasons or for no reason at all, murders were committed, some making national and international headlines. Eleven are recalled here, four of them committed by teenagers, two causing the death of a boy and two involving that most mercurial of all elements in a murder – chance. Shootings brought about by anger, jealousy, the need for money and the need to assault a woman, killed four more local people. Of the others, an elderly lady was, perhaps, suffocated, and another was bludgeoned to death with an iron bar. Battering, the most bloody of the deaths and the only one here for which the murderer is still sought, killed a young woman solicitor from London who just happened, inexplicably, to be driving through.

Other crimes, if not murder, make equally fascinating reading. A gang of Cambridge men conspired to safebreak and burgle, while other non-local gangs used the areas road system to drive in and out to commit their crimes – eluding the police to carry out numerous silver, art and antiques raids, and eluding the Flying Squad in their attempt to hijack a cash-in-transit van.

The area's police officers were directly involved when the black eyes were being handed out in two riot situations, one in Cambridge, when politically roused university students laid siege to a hotel, and one in Newmarket, when striking stablelads tried to prevent the Guineas taking place at the Rowley Mile racecourse.

Two of the criminals brought to justice here were each unique in their own way, breathtaking in their sheer audacity and self-belief – the self-styled 'Major', a master conman who knew how to tell a story and how to acquire other people's money, and the most infamous wrongdoer ever to have been born, raised and gone wrong in the city, the Cambridge Rapist.

You will enjoy reading about them all.

CHAPTER 1

Too Mean to Live

1956

She gave a gurgle and stopped breathing

Rachel Mary Parsons, born in 1885, was a remarkable, brilliant woman, and could have been more so had the male-dominated norms of the day allowed her to be. She was the daughter of Sir Charles Parsons, the inventor of the marine steam turbine, and she inherited his love of and talent for engineering. Not the thing for a Victorian young lady.

Rachel became the first woman to study mechanical engineering at the University of Cambridge where she distinguished herself. She went on to become a qualified marine engineer, the only woman to hold a master mariner's ticket, was president of the Women's Engineering Society and one of the few women associates of the Institute of Naval Architects.

All of that she had intended would lead her to a place in the family engineering business, which she was given during the First World War while her brother fought for his country. When he was killed, it seemed that the way was open for her position to become permanent but, when the war ended, there was no job for her.

She was a woman. Her place was in the home. She chose the man she wanted to marry, to make that home with, but her parents did not approve. And young ladies, then, did their parents' bidding. She did not marry him.

Rachel became a member of London County Council and a parliamentary candidate, hoping to become a member of parliament. But that did not happen. So she became a 'woman about town'. With an apartment in Grosvenor Square, London, Miss Parsons became known for her love of expensive fast cars and for being a society hostess, her glittering parties attended by the rich, famous and royal.

In 1931, on the death of her father, she inherited £840,000 and was reputed to be the fifth richest person in Britain. Leaving Grosvenor Square, she bought the lease of a large house in Belgrave Square. It had its own ballroom but, by 1939 and the start of the Second World War, she had given her last party. She lived alone and, after a burglary, moved elsewhere in the Square. But, perhaps a little concerned that she was alone, she began to prefer to stay in hotels.

Her love of animals – horses in particular – became greater and, in 1947, she bought a thirty-seven bedroom mansion and stables, Branches Park, in wooded grounds at Cowlinge, near Newmarket, Suffolk, one of the largest estates in the country. Going into horse racing, she spent large amounts of money buying, breeding and racing thoroughbreds, her pale blue and mauve colours becoming well known on the racecourse, often in the winner's enclosure.

Miss Parsons, by then in her sixties, had become very different from the party giver who had made Mayfair her own. She was known in and around Newmarket for her eccentricity. She entertained nobody at Branches Park. Unable to keep staff because of her unpleasantness, she lived in two squalid rooms and those who did step inside the mansion told stories of fodder and potatoes stored in large, once-luxurious rooms, and dirt and disarray everywhere.

The mansion, with no staff to care for it and no money spent on it, settled into disrepair, eight cars rusting in its garages while Miss Parsons, who lost her driving licence in 1953, took taxis. The trailblazer, the heiress, the sparkler of the 1920s and 1930s, had become a scruffy old lady in a shabby coat, down-at-heel mud-caked shoes, socks with holes in, a capacious handbag and a large 'fruit salad' hat. Always the hat.

Miss Parsons loved animals, but she had little liking for people and no respect. She was foul-tempered and foul-mouthed. As Charles Bell, one of her succession of trainers said: 'Most people were either a rat or a guttersnipe to her. She called me everything and I think she knew every word in the dictionary. I lost three stone while I was in her employ.' He had lasted longer than most. Nine months. In the year before her death she went through three trainers.

Difficulty in finding a trainer forced Miss Parsons to buy a property in Newmarket, in a cul-de-sac off the top of the High Street, close to the heath and the Rowley Mile racecourse. Her once seventy or so strong string much reduced, she installed her horses at Lansdowne House, living again in only a couple of rooms. At the time of her death, in July 1956, she had no trainer for her ten horses and just four stablemen to care for them.

Former Landsdowne House, Newmarket. The author

The favourite and best of her horses was *Le Dieu d'Or*. Until early May of 1956 it had been cared for by a twenty-six-year-old ex-apprentice jockey, Dennis James Pratt, a married man with two children and a third on the way. He had left unable to take any more of its owner's irascibility.

The short distance from Landsdowne House to Newmarket Heath. The author

Miss Parsons owned other property and houses in the area and over recent years she had been involved in numerous court cases because of her failure to carry out repairs. Warnings and heavy fines had little effect. She was vehemently opposed to paying out money for anything or anyone. One pleasure that she did allow herself was to visit the cinema in Cambridge. She would take a taxi the twelve miles to Cambridge two or three times a week, sometimes keeping it waiting outside until the show was over. There was always more than enough money in her handbag to pay for those trips. She seemed not to quibble over the cost of her taxis but every other payment she did quibble over. She always knew exactly how much she owed, down to last penny, but she would oppose to the death her obligation to make that payment.

And that is what she did.

On the evening of Sunday 1 July, Dennis Pratt went to Lansdowne House to see Miss Parsons about the two weeks' holiday money he claimed that she owed him. It was not his first visit for the same purpose. He had left Miss Parsons employ on 4 May but had been seen about the stable yard since that date, asking for his money. She had informed the police on one occasion. On 21 May Detective Sergeant Ronald Bigmore of the Newmarket police told Pratt not to visit Lansdowne House or to pester Miss Parsons and he promised to keep away. But he broke his promise.

At the end of June, Miss Parsons took a taxi from Cambridge railway station to Lansdowne House, a journey its driver was later to recall when Pratt appeared before Newmarket magistrates accused of her wilful murder:

'We arrived at about 10-45 am and saw Pratt at the front door. Miss Parsons got out of the taxi and I heard her say, "What are you doing here? I will ring the police and have you arrested." Pratt said, "I have come to see you about my two weeks holiday money. I have got no money."'

She did tell the police and Bigmore repeated his warning to Pratt to keep away from Lansdowne House. He chose, again, not to do so. Regrettably, just a few days later, he called again.

Pratt's own words, in a statement made to Cambridge City Police the next day, Monday 2 July, tell what happened next:

'I went back to the house last night to get my holiday money and I saw Miss Parsons. I asked her for my money and she hit me with her handbag. She hit me a couple of times and I shouted at her for her to stop. I picked up an iron bar. She carried on going for me with her handbag and I carried on with the iron bar.'

He went on to tell police, graphically, the unfolding of what seemed to him, later, 'all like a bad dream':

She went down on the shingle. I picked her up by the shoulders and she was bleeding slightly. I did not know what to do. I sat with her and held her head. I did not know whether to run away or not. I could not help her and then I realised it was too late to help her. She gave a gurgle and stopped breathing. I got her into the house. I went upstairs and with the keys I had taken from her handbag I unlocked the bedroom door. I was trying to make my mind up what to do. I remembered her handbag and went into the saddle room and took the money from the bag. In the bedroom again I took some binoculars, two small glass ornaments and some beads. After locking up the room I went downstairs and put her in the pantry. I went through the house, locked the doors behind me and locked the back door. I took the bar I had hit her with and put it in the back yard.

'It was getting light and I think it was 3 o'clock in the morning and I went home and had a cup of tea. My wife was asleep. I went to bed and got up again at 6 o'clock. After having a cup of tea I cycled up to Lansdowne House and went to the pantry. She was still lying in the same position. I put out a light which I left on because she always slept with it on. I

Portland Road, Newmarket today. The author

relocked the doors and kicked the shingle where there was some blood. I threw the iron bar on the coke under the stairs. I went home.

I told my wife I had been to get a paper. The kettle was boiling so I made a cup of tea. It was about 6-45. I waited in the house about five minutes and then went into Newmarket. I had a cup of tea in a restaurant and bought some chocolate which I gave to my wife and daughter. I then put my raincoat on but not my jacket because of blood on the front. I hitch-hiked to Cambridge and tried to sell the binoculars.

And that was what had got him into the police station in Cambridge.

Once in Cambridge, he had gone from shop to shop trying to sell his stolen goods. Besides the binoculars he had a couple of cameras and travelling clocks in a brown leather attache case. About 12-30 pm he went into Fred Morley and Co, jewellers and silversmiths, where the assistant at once had doubts that the

Morley's jewellers and pawnbrokers, Cambridge. Cambridgeshire Collection

expensive binoculars were Pratt's to sell. Pratt said that they were his late father's and that he was selling them for his mother, but he could prove nothing, not even his name and address. He had given a false name. He was asked to leave the binoculars for valuation and to call back after lunch. When he went back Cambridge City detectives followed him into the shop.

Believing that they had their hands on a suspicious character with stolen goods, too much paper money in his wallet and no verifiable ID, they took him in for further questioning. They got more than they bargained for when, during questioning, Pratt became upset and sobbed: 'This will be a shock to you. I have done her in.'

They were shocked.

Too emotional to write his own statement, he dictated it to Detective Constable Kenneth Proctor who, remarking that he had already given two false names and addresses, asked him if he was telling the truth when he said that he had killed Rachel Parsons by hitting her on the head with an iron bar. He assured them that he was, and Proctor saw then the state of Pratt's trousers.

'I noticed a reddish brown stain below the left knee of his grey flannel trousers. There was another small stain on the right leg near the turn-up.'

Pratt said: 'I think that is blood from her head when I tried to lift her.'

A call was put through to police in Newmarket while Pratt continued his statement. His statement had begun at 2-30 pm and it was 5-30 pm before it was finished, but at 4-15 pm Newmarket police called back to the police in Cambridge. A body had been found.

Detective Sergeant Bigmore had gone to Lansdowne House with two other officers at 2-40 pm and had found all the doors and windows locked. Detective Constable Connolly had managed to get in through a cellar flap. He had then broken open a door at the top of the cellar steps to get into the kitchen and then he had let his fellow officers into the house by the lobby door. They found the inhabited rooms 'in a big muddle' with stale food and rubbish lying about and the carpets filthy.

They then forced the door of the larder and, behind a screen, they found the body of Rachel Parsons under 'various wrappings'. An overcoat covered the top of her body. A sack covered her head and another sack was round her legs and feet. Her shoes were next to her head, but she still wore her hat, a black one, knocked to the back of her head by the blows that had fractured her skull or perhaps, thoughtfully, replaced. Death had, however, parted her from her handbag. That was found in the front hall, at the foot of the stairs. After a search, the iron bar was found in the coke cupboard of the drying room of the bottom stable. One end was bloodstained.

The police went to Pratt's home in nearby Portland Road at 5-35 pm and, after breaking into a shed, they found a tin containing a gold-coloured powder compact, a white glass and metal powder compact, three strings of pearls, one necklace of amber beads and another of glass. All were of little value. On a table were a bloodstained jacket and the keys to Lansdowne House.

Two hours later, Bigmore was at Cambridge police station arresting Pratt for murder.

Newmarket Magistrates twice remanded Pratt, the second occasion, on 10 July, being perhaps memorable for being only the second time ever that a London press photographer was accused by police of taking a photograph within the precincts of the court. Charles Ley of the *Daily Mirror* was said to have hidden a camera under a raincoat and hankie. A faint click was heard. Ley was brought before Newmarket magistrates but got

Newmarket General Hospital. The author

away with it because he had not got a photograph. Had the police charged him with trying to take a photograph he could have been found guilty. As it was, the case was dismissed. But the incident shows the national interest in the murder. It was a very big story.

An inquest into the death of Miss Parsons was carried out by the coroner for the Liberty of Bury St Edmunds, Mr T Wilson, with evidence of identification being given by Frederick Scallon, a stud groom at Branches Park, who said that he had seen her every day, except when there was racing at Epsom or Ascot. Dr Colin Walker, who had been called to Lansdowne House by the police after the discovery of the murder, said that the body had been in a large cupboard near the back door and that her only injury had been to the head. She had then been dead between twelve and twenty-four hours. The inquest had then been adjourned until 23 October.

A post-mortem on the body of Rachel Parsons was carried out at Newmarket General Hospital on the afternoon of 3 July by Dr Francis Camps, the distinguished but unpopular Home Office forensic pathologist and Professor of Forensic Medicine at London University, known for the speed and arrogant skill with which he worked. He must have hit the small Newmarket morgue like a whirlwind. He found a trivial graze on the right cheek, bruises on the left centre lower lip, three lacerated wounds on the side of the scalp associated with fracture of the skull, and bruising of the brain and haemorrhage. The lacerations were characteristic of those due to a linear object.

When Pratt was tried at Essex Assizes in Chelmsford on 13 November, Camps, shown the iron bar, said that it could 'quite definitely' have caused the injuries. Pratt was defended by the ebullient bon viveur Michael Havers, father of actor Nigel. Vigorous in court, and later having a highly successful political career, Havers said that he would be asking for a verdict of manslaughter. Addressing the jury, he said that the fact that Pratt had taken various articles from the dead woman's house must not be considered. Miss Parsons was clearly a bitter and vindictive woman. That was evident by the way she had called Pratt 'a guttersnipe'.

She had. Moments before Pratt had raised the bar to her head she had called both him and his wife guttersnipes. And she had called him 'a tramp'.

Summing up, Mr Justice Diplock said: 'If you are satisfied that there was provocation on the part of the deceased then the

verdict would be one of manslaughter.' He said that the jury had
been given a picture of a strange, unpleasant, quarrelsome
woman who was quick to abuse.

Of Pratt, he said that he had struck her, not once but three
times, with a bar of iron and with such force that her skull was
fractured in two places. The second and third blows were
probably struck as she fell. He had then dragged her body into
the house and had gone home for a cup of tea. The following
day he had gone back to the house and had put out the lights
and had then gone to Cambridge to sell the things he had taken.

Justice Diplock concluded with: 'These are the acts of a
pretty cool customer.'

The jury took two hours and twenty minutes to return a
verdict of manslaughter. In sentencing a sobbing Pratt to ten
years imprisonment Diplock said: 'You killed an old woman in
a most brutal fashion. The jury have taken a merciful view of
your case, but that cannot disguise the fact that this was a very
brutal crime.'

Rachel Parsons' cousin, Canon R E Parsons, Warden of
Moore Park College, Farnham, officiated at her funeral at St

Newmarket Cemetery. The author

Mary's church, Newmarket, on 6 July. It was attended by about fifty family and other mourners who stood about in small groups in the church grounds until the cortege arrived. All of the family mourners, led by the Earl and Countess of Rosse, were cousins of the deceased. They then went on to Newmarket Cemetery, just across the High Street from the scene of her murder, for her interment. The cemetery was closed to the public and both gates were guarded by police. A number of curious spectators watched over the cemetery wall as the last rites were administered to, surely, one of racing's most eccentric characters.

A firm of London solicitors was engaged to administer Miss Parsons' considerable estate. She had died intestate and, as a member of the firm said: 'So far as we are aware no will has ever been found and it is assumed that none has ever been made.'

When Branches Park was sold, soon after, the mansion, which had stood since 1739, was in such a derelict state that it had to be demolished.

Lansdowne House later became a nursing home, providing more comfort for the elderly than it had given to Rachel Parsons.

CHAPTER 2

Death of a Gypsy

1960

*Still alive, she was battered about the head
with the butt of the shotgun . . .*

There had been days of rain. A headline on the front
page of the local newspaper, *Cambridge Independent
Press,* on Friday 15 July 1960 was: START ON
HARVEST IN A FEW DAYS. Most cereal crops
promised well, the item stated, but 'Barley is the most worrying
crop at the moment because the wet weather has beaten it
down.' Above was a bigger, blacker headline: SHOT
WOMAN'S BODY FOUND IN CORN-FIELD. The dead
woman had run into a field of barley trying, and failing, to
escape her killer. The barley was beaten down around her body,
but not by the weather.

Cambridge is surrounded by cornfields, rich arable lands that,
close to the fertile fens, also produce an abundance of strawber-
ries and other fruits. Histon was a perfect location for Chivers to
have a jam factory. Ethel Harriet Collinge had a job there, as did
many local women. In her mid-40s, she lived at Westwick
Cottages in the Cambridgeshire village of Oakington with her
husband, Donald, who was a civilian batman at the airfield close
to the village, RAF Oakington. They had a sixteen-year-old son.

Her body was found close to a footpath which villagers used
as a short cut between Histon and Oakington.

A woman who knew Mrs Collinge told a Cambridgeshire
coroner's inquest on 22 July: 'She used to catch the 8-05 train
from Oakington to Histon every morning. Until recently she
came back by train in the early afternoon, but when that train
was stopped running she used her cycle. Sometimes she came
by the main road but on three or four occasions she used the
short cut.'

A fellow worker, Mrs Ida Mary Stearn, said that on the day
of the murder she cycled part of the way home with Mrs
Collinge. 'She said she was going along the footpath because it
was a long way round the airfield.'

The footpath ran about fifty yards from the Cambridge to March railway line, with a dyke, trees and a small wood on one side and a field of barley belonging to Westwick Hall Farm on the other. In wet weather it got very muddy in places. Mrs Collinge had doubts about using it that Wednesday. It was a nice day, with sun at last, but it would take a while to dry out.

As she set off along the path she met a boy, fourteen-year-old Raymond Mahoney, going back to school after lunch. He said: 'I saw Mrs Collinge coming up the path on her cycle near a water tank. We passed each other and Mrs Collinge asked me: 'Is it wet down there?' and she carried on.'

Moments earlier, Raymond Mahoney had heard a voice coming from the trees beside the footpath. It had called: 'Come here.' He had thought that it was the voice of Gypsy Jack Smith, but he could see no one and so he had gone on.

Gypsy Jack Smith was known to hide in trees. It was later thought that, on that day, he had swung down in front of Mrs Collinge from his hiding place in a tree and had blocked her way.

What had then taken place, leading up to the moment of her

RAF Oakington. Cambridgeshire Collection

death, police could only surmise. But, from the start, Gypsy Jack was the number one suspect. He had to be found, quickly. To that end, the Cambridgeshire County Police began the biggest manhunt in its history and called in the Scotland Yard murder squad, led by Superintendent John du Rose. His speed in cracking cases had earned him the nickname of Five Days Johnny. By early 1965, when he investigated, but on that occasion did not solve in five days, the eight Thames-side killings of London prostitutes by a murderer nicknamed Jack the Stripper, he had become Deputy Assistant Commissioner of the Metropolitan Police.

Thorough police work would be needed to find the killer of Ethel Collinge and, as du Rose stated at the inquest, that is what he got. And not only from the Yard men. 'I found the Cambridgeshire force well-trained and as efficient as any force in the country. Many of the men worked their full shift and volunteered to go out again with dogs. They made endless inquiries and were tireless in their desire to find the killer.'

William 'Gypsy Jack' Smith, in his early twenties, lived with his mother, Violet, in a knocked-together dwelling that was part-greenhouse, part-hut and part-old railway carriage in a gypsy encampment on the Cottenham road in Oakington. A blonded, swaggering petty criminal with a stolen shotgun, he had been sought by police for five weeks before the killing of Mrs Collinge. He was on probation for attacking another woman as she had cycled home from work. He had been due to appear at Cambridge City Quarter Sessions on 3 June for breaching that probation but, on his way to court, he had disappeared.

The scene, the pathologist, and Mrs Collinge herself, told the police what had probably taken place. Confronted by Gypsy Jack, a gun in her face, Mrs Collinge had dropped her cycle and had run along the footpath, losing her shoes as she went, running through the mud she had been so keen to avoid. She dropped her handbag. If it was money he wanted perhaps he would leave her alone once he had her handbag. He still followed her. She went into the barley field, beside a clump of trees.

About forty-five yards into the barley she was shot in the left side of her back, and then she was shot again at close range. Still alive, she was then battered about the head with the butt of the shotgun and, finally, she was raped.

When Gypsy Jack left her he took her bag and her green shoes, later found by police. Det Insp Percy Fouracre of the Cambridgeshire force, assisting du Rose, said: 'We found a handbag stuffed down a rabbit hole in the wood. It has been taken away for examination together with its contents.'

Michael Carpenter, a fifteen-year-old Oakington schoolboy, telling the inquest that he and Gypsy Jack used to cycle about the village together, proved to be a vital witness. Of the time before the murder he said: 'I remember cycling along the Cottenham road when Jack called to me. I went to him. He had his 12-bore shotgun. He told me the police were looking for him and we arranged to meet the next night. On our second meeting, he said he had got the gun from Peterborough. When I met him later he let me shoot at a cellophane bag. Afterwards he asked me if I could get him any cartridges. I got them straight away from a shop in Oakington. I also got him some cakes and cigarettes.'

Carpenter arranged to meet Gypsy Jack again. Their next meeting was to be on 12 July, the day of the murder, a meeting he was unlikely to forget. 'I left school and came home along the footpath. I saw Jack Smith on the footpath, near a railway carriage. He was carrying his gun under his arm. He caught me up and we had a cigarette. While we were walking along he said: "I've killed a woman", but I said I did not believe him. He said, "I've got her shoes and bag." He took them from behind a big tree and showed them to me. Jack opened the bag and took out the purse.'

Police reported that there was no money in the purse when examined by them. It had contained a £1 note.

'A savings book fell out and he put them back. We went back on the footpath and Jack asked me if I wanted to see the woman. I said: "No". Jack told me: "I did it because she had me put inside before." He saw I was frightened and said he would put his gun down and walk a little way with me. Then he asked me to get him a shovel saying: "I want to get rid of the woman and her bike", but I said: "No". He took a £1 note from his wallet and held it out to me and asked me if I could get some more cartridges for him, but I again said: "No". That was the last I saw of him.'

Gypsy Jack did not get a shovel.

Mrs Collinge had left work at 1pm. When her husband got home from work at RAF Oakington in the evening she was not there. He said: 'Later in the evening I looked for her along the footpath. She usually came that way if it was fine.' He did not find her or her bike. At midnight he reported to police that she had not returned home.

A neighbour in Westwick Cottages, Frank Prior, joined the search for her the next day and he found a bicycle, a blue sports cycle, which he thought was hers. Soon after, seeing the track made into the barley field, PC Arthur Peck, based at

Cottenham, made the discovery everyone had been dreading.

He told the inquest: 'I found the body of Mrs Collinge in some growing barley. It was lying on its back and was scantily dressed. The corn around the body was flattened.'

In a quiet rural area where people knew each other, which Oakington still was despite the airfield, Gypsy Jack had made himself noticed and disliked. The police had little difficulty in amassing information against him.

Many people had shotguns in Oakington and used them with respect. Cartridges were easily come by and as easily used, but properly. Pigeon shooting was a village pastime. But Gypsy Jack played about with his shotgun. He toted it, sometimes wearing a bandolier of cartridges. He fancied himself with it. He was the local bad boy, the local ruffian.

The gun used to kill Mrs Collinge had been stolen from a hut on some allotments at Rampton about a month before. Smith was a known thief – and he had committed sexual offences. The police had been certain, almost from the start, that he was their man but, as on his way to court five weeks before, he had disappeared. He had gone to ground.

Du Rose felt that he would not be far from his gypsy encampment of broken-down huts. It had been searched several times and he had not been found, but that did not change his view. Predictably, no one at the camp had seen him or knew his whereabouts. It must be searched yet again in a surprise raid.

A distraction was staged. Something to make a wanted man feel a little bit less cornered. Sixty police officers, some from other forces, and helped by twelve dogs, moved openly through orchards and fields – but the sweep they made was away from Smith's encampment. Meanwhile, a second group of forty hand-picked men quietly got together on Cottenham Green, about a mile from the encampment, and prepared for action. They swooped in, swiftly and unexpectedly. They would scour the place, inch by inch, and they were even equipped to search underground. They had spades and they would dig him out if necessary.

Gypsy Jack's mother, Violet, squatted by the roadside close to the home she and her son shared as the police made ready to search it yet again. Not the best place to sit when, if found, Gypsy Jack might try to shoot himself out. For her safety she was put into a police van and taken to police headquarters as the search of the hut began.

There was little enough of the makeshift home. It was obvious that Gypsy Jack was not there. For all their speed and surprise, the police had drawn a blank, at his home at least. They would continue throughout the camp. The police at the Smith home made ready to move on. And then, as he went outside with some of Gypsy Jack's belongings, PC Ronald Roberts noticed something. The inside of the hut was shorter than the outside.

Du Rose and Fouracre pulled away a chest of drawers from an old wooden partition, its boards mouldy with age. It was secured, nailed together, no one was meant to have got in or out, but du Rose managed to tear some of the boards away until he could poke his head through the gap he had made. A somewhat foolhardy thing to do because there was Gypsy Jack sitting in the dark, in his secret compartment.

There was just enough light for du Rose to be able to see the fully-loaded shotgun he held, his finger ready on the trigger. But he did not blast du Rose. He shot himself. As du Rose thrust himself through the gap Gypsy Jack's arm slowly dropped to touch the floor.

By the time more police officers broke through the partition and into the secret hideout Gypsy Jack lay dead on the floor, his shotgun across his chest.

After his body was taken away, wrapped in a blanket, sunlight began to brighten the blackness of his tomb-like hideaway to show an old table, a chipped washbowl, two cups and a half-eaten sandwich. There was a faded painting on the wall and a yellow plaid rug on the floor.

When du Rose came out from examining the tiny space his hands and suit were covered in blood.

The shotgun, with one live cartridge in the breech, which could so easily have been used to kill du Rose, was put into a police car along with a bandolier of fourteen live cartridges and taken away.

The search for the killer of Ethel Harriet Collinge was over, five days after her murder. Du Rose had lived up to his nickname of Five Days Johnny.

At the joint inquest into the two deaths the Cambridgeshire coroner, Mr V O D Cade, said to Insp Fouracre: 'The witness Carpenter said Smith told him this woman had got him inside on an earlier occasion. Have you followed this up?'

Fouracre replied: 'I am satisfied that this woman was in no way connected with his previous offences.'

After a brief retirement, the jury decided that Mrs Collinge had been murdered by William 'Gypsy Jack' Smith who had then committed suicide when about to be arrested.

More than 200 people attended Mrs Collinge's funeral at Oakington parish church on Wednesday 20 July, only a week after her murder. A lorry was needed to carry seventy wreaths. Both du Rose and Fouracre paid their last respects to the woman they had only got to know in death but had done their best to justify.

Gypsies came from miles around to pay their last respects at the funeral of Gypsy Jack.

St Andrew's Church, Oakington. The author

CHAPTER 3

Let Me Tell you a Story

1963–64

. . . the supreme confidence trickster

There is something breathtaking about the master confidence trickster. Something awesome in the sheer scale and scope of the scams and the panache with which they are carried out when most of us would look furtive if we found we had been given a pound too much in our change and kept it.

Forty-two-year-old Michael Patrick Murphy Woodfall, self-styled retired Royal Horse Artillery major and bloodstock dealer of great wealth and property, was such a man. Over the years he had preyed upon many victims, most of them women with a bit of money. Effie Ora was to be his last.

Mrs Elizabeth 'Effie' Ora was an attractive fifty-year-old widow living in Histon, a mile or so to the north of Cambridge. Lonely after the death of her businessman husband, Steve, she was introduced to Woodfall through a matrimonial agency.

Their first meeting was outside a Cambridge cinema in the spring of 1963 and from their first moments together he began to spin stories of his wartime work as a spycatcher, his service in the Royal Horse Artillery, his job, his wealth, his titled relatives, his property in Cornwall and his house and estate in Ireland.

From all that he told her Mrs Ora soon believed him to be 'well connected' and thought herself lucky to have met such a charming, well spoken man, distinguished with his rampant moustache and military bearing.

Mrs Ora had done some talking too. From what she had told him Woodfall knew that her husband had left her and her seventeen-year-old daughter, Rosemary, financially secure and he quickly decided that it could be to his advantage to continue the friendship. Within three days of that first meeting he had proposed marriage and, after he had told her in detail of his annual income of £30,000 from his work for the British Bloodstock Agency, his £17,000 from a trust fund and his stately ancestral home in Co Galway, she accepted.

He told her that he was a single man. He had never married, but he had once been in love. It had ended tragically. She had served in Intelligence with him early in World War Two and had been parachuted into France. She had been shot when she landed. He had never got over it and had coped at the time by keeping himself occupied, mostly by escaping from prisoner-of-war camps in Japan and Germany, including Belsen, working for MI5 and helping the Maquis.

On 29 April they were married and, almost at once, Woodfall borrowed £2,000 from his bride. After that, they were often seen about the hotels and bars of Cambridge, Woodfall so plausibly spinning his stories to fascinated audiences, including Effie. He could certainly tell a story. He gave her a cheque for £20,000, but asked her not to cash it until his affairs in Ireland were sorted out. He said that he meant to give a considerable sum to Rosemary when she became twenty-one. In the meantime, a joint bank account would be a good idea.

They went to Ireland for the summer, driving there in a hired, chauffeur-driven Rolls Royce, paid for by Effie. In Galway, he took the new Mrs Woodfall to visit his ancestral home, Bermingham House, a slightly dilapidated large country house in impressive grounds. There were paintings of his ancestors on the walls, and Effie could see the family likeness, only – they were all called Cusack-Smith. His mother's side of the family, Woodfall explained. Lady Cusack-Smith had been housekeeper there for his family for twenty years, but now the house was his, and it was to be Effie's wedding present.

They whirled themselves into the social life of the area, on occasion flying back to Cambridge for parties or race meetings or for Woodfall to attend the bloodstock sales in Newmarket. Woodfall became keen on the local hunt and got himself involved with the 'horsey' set. They went to the Dublin Horse Show and it was there that three times Effie heard Woodfall deny that he was renting Bermingham House from its owner Lady Cusack-Smith. Obviously some mistake, of course it was his, and he had given it to her as a wedding present, although – she had heard Lady Cusack-Smith herself speak of 'my house'.

Woodfall said that he had a surprise for Effie, a bigger surprise than Bermingham House. Now that he was coming home, coming into his own, he had decided to revert to his title. He was Sir Patrick Murphy Woodfall. He had not used the title before, he told Lady Effie, because his mother had taken a vow of poverty and it was for her sake.

Effie would have been even more surprised had she known, then, that that was only the latest in a series of incarnations. Her husband could just as brashly have announced himself as Sir Patrick Johnson, son of Lord Manchester, Captain George Johnson of MI5, Lieutenant Roland Jones of the Australian Secret Service, Major Michael Woodfall DSO MC, managing director of splendid hotels in Cornwall, or the Honourable Michael Duckworth, public schoolboy.

Known in top society as much for his bouncing cheques as his name, whatever it was, on a previous visit to Ireland he had put it about that he was Colonel Sir Patrick Murphy, ex-Governor of the Bahamas. Welcomed into the Dublin top set, he had borrowed money without repayment and, as usual, had courted the wealthy ladies.

So many, along the way and over the years, were taken in by the outlandish exploits and stories Woodfall recounted that it could seem beyond credibility. Why was he believed without question by so many people? But then, perhaps it was the confidence he put into the confidence trick that did it. The bizarre fact that the governor of a prison where Woodfall was being held came to believe that he was really with MI5 and was in prison working undercover shows the calibre of the man. He was a master of his art.

Effie Ora from Histon did not stand a chance.

But just who and what had she met, fallen in love with and married?

He was Patrick Johnson, born in Mandalay in 1921, the son of an army officer who died in Burma before his birth. He was brought up by an uncle, an officer in the Indian Army. Educated in England, he was expelled from two public schools, already a hopeless case, a conman and a thief.

If he had paid more attention to his education he might, as he so intensely wished, have got into Sandhurst and become an army officer. But that was one place no story could get him into. The best he could manage was the Royal Artillery where he served through World War Two as a lowly gunner. He was never more than a gunner.

His only chance of the promotion he yearned for was to do it for himself. And it was easy. He made himself Second Lieutenant Sir Patrick Johnson, the nineteen year old son of Lord Manchester, and he celebrated his commission with a champagne party at the *Savoy Hotel* in London. He left his party with what was to become a trademark exit. He left without paying the bill.

A similar stunt in Bath was not so successful. It landed him in Borstal for three years, where he learned more than he ever could at the best schools in the land, or at Sandhurst. He learned how to be the best at his chosen profession, the supreme confidence trickster. He emerged from Borstal a new man – a much-decorated hero of the war, spycatcher Captain George Johnson of MI5.

It was then, and in that persona, that he met and enchanted his first wealthy widow.

The scams, the false pretences, the tall stories, the fiancées, followed thick and fast. As did, inevitably, the prison sentences. When Woodfall met Effie in Cambridge he had spent nineteen years of his life in prison and had just been released after nine years 'preventive detention' in Dartmoor.

Strangely, he did tell her about that, but not the true story that he had parted a Hatton Garden jeweller from his £600 diamond brooch, had fled to Ireland and had been arrested after being seen on television, the dashing ex-Governor of the Bahamas, dancing at a ball with his Irish bride-to-be. He had been arrested after being recognised by police in London as their old friend 'Champagne Charlie'.

The story he told Effie soon after they met, urged on, with Woodfall's knack for the unusual, by a Catholic priest in a Sussex guest house, was that he had been engaged to a secretary at one of his Cornish hotels and she had always wanted expensive jewellery. Taking her out to dinner one evening, he had borrowed jewellery, including a very expensive brooch, for her to wear. During dinner she had broken it to him that she was already married, which had upset him so much that, not knowing what he was doing, he had taken the boat to Ireland with the brooch in his pocket.

Telling Effie that murky secret in his past, that, however undeservedly, he had been a Dartmoor resident, disturbed him intensely, so much so that he threatened suicide, sure that he would lose the woman he loved. He assured her that that was the only trouble he had ever been in, and she thought that, given the circumstances, he had been hard done by. Nine years! A frightful sentence, and all over a misunderstanding. She reassured him that it would make no difference at all to their relationship.

She was in love, and her life with Woodfall was certainly on the up. She was no longer the lonely widow from Histon. He was going to present her to the Queen at a Royal Ball at Windsor Castle. That was about as up as it could get. But the curtsies worried her. Would she be able to get it right? She practised and practised. She need not have bothered. When they were at Royal Ascot he was called to the stewards' office and given a telegram – from himself – to tell him that his titled aunt had died. He must go into mourning at once and travel to Trowbridge for the funeral. Sadly, there could be no Royal Ball.

Effie was aware, while at Ascot, that Woodfall was arranging a mortgage of £6,000 on two-thirds of her residuary estate. If she was not concerned about the part Woodfall was playing in her finances her solicitor was.

Mr H W Kester of the long-established Cambridge firm of Few and Kester, a friend of Effie's late husband, had been entrusted with the management of his estate and the future financial security of his widow and daughter. He was concerned at the way Mrs Ora's new husband, although claiming to be a wealthy man, was taking over control of her money and spending it. Letters were exchanged but she chose to ignore his concerns and advice. Persuaded by Woodfall, she falsely accused Kester of mismanaging her finances and dispensed with his services, stating that her new husband's 'past, present and future are entirely known to me'.

She could hardly have been more wrong.

Shortly after the non-event of the Royal Ball, a friend of Effie's began to have doubts about the dashing new man in her life. From childhood, the son and nephew of a military family, Woodfall had been obsessed by all things military. He had an encyclopaedic knowledge of the British Army and especially of his supposed regiment, the Royal Horse Artillery. But the inexplicable happened. Effie's friend knew a bit about the RHA herself and, in conversation with Woodfall, he had not known something that every RHA man must know. It would be useless to tell Effie. She would not listen. Instead, her friend told another friend who happened to be a police officer, in CID. A casual mention of the larger-than-life major brought the police into Woodfall's life yet again.

In July and August the police called on Woodfall when he and Effie were staying at a hotel in London, and Detective Chief Inspector Joseph Breed of the Cambridge police visited him at Effie's home in Histon.

What was revealed in those interviews tore at the very roots of Effie's relationship with Woodfall and shattered her unquestioning belief in him. She was staggered to hear that her husband's name was not Woodfall but Johnson, that he had been

The former city centre police station, Cambridge. The author

a gunner in the Royal Artillery and never a major in the Royal Horse Artillery, that he did not work for the British Bloodstock Agency, that he had no money and no property, and that in Bristol in 1942 he had married Brenda Wright. There was no record of a divorce.

He said that he loved Effie. 'I wouldn't hurt a hair of her head. I have told her lies about property and the Army, but it is not a criminal offence to tell lies.'

But, at last, she was seeing him for what he was. He had lost his shine. Most of all, she regretted sacking the solicitor her late husband had been right to trust. She realised, belatedly, how foolish she had been to let Woodfall, a 'wholly unscrupulous adventurer', extract thousands of pounds from her. She would admit as much at Woodfall's trial and offer Kester an apology.

Above: *Jockey Club, Newmarket*. The author
Above inset: *Entrance to Jockey Club office, Newmarket*. The author

When Effie told Woodfall it was all over he threatened suicide, and he even tried it, carefully. He sent her flowers and bombarded her with calls, at her door and on the phone. She would not be moved. It was over while she still had some of her fortune left.

Used to wowing and wooing the many ladies whose paths he crossed, and perhaps, as he said, genuinely fond of Effie, he found rejection hard to take, but he had almost reached the end of a long and muddy road.

He was arrested by Cambridge police and charged with obtaining sums totalling £5,900, later reduced to £4,400, from Mrs Ora by false pretences. He was also charged with making a false statement in order to marry her. In other words, he had committed bigamy.

He spent the night in Bedford prison and was taken back to Cambridge the next morning to be remanded in custody. It was then that he staged his grand finale as the master conman he was. He arrived at Cambridge police station in a taxi, handcuffed and with a police escort. The police station, at that time, was in a busy street in the heart of town. As he got out of the taxi he bolted into the crowds.

Managing to work free of his handcuffs, he found a taxi and was away on his last flight, or drive, of fancy. He went twelve miles to Newmarket where he called at the Jockey Club to get race entry forms for his non-existent horses. He then went on to Royston to persuade a well known trainer to take on his string of non-existent horses. He agreed. He and the taxi driver stayed in Royston for a fine lunch, with his favourite oysters, and then he was off to London. He did not leave a tip. Neither did he pay the bill.

In London, he called at the Royal Automobile Club and then he and the taxi driver had champagne at the bar of a Piccadilly hotel where he said he was to meet another racehorse trainer. After that, he told his driver, they would be on their way back to Cambridge. He went to the Gents and disappeared.

And, shortly after that, the major's luck turned against him. He booked into one of the hundreds of small, nondescript hotels in Paddington and it was reminiscent of a scene in the film *Casablanca*, where Humphrey Bogart says something about 'of all the gin joints in all the towns in all the world she walks into mine'. Of all the hotels in Paddington to choose from Woodfall had walked into that one.

The hotel's owners were from Ireland. They had run a hotel

in County Mayo seven years before. They knew Woodfall. They recognised him at once and they knew that he was a wanted man. The next morning he went down to more than a full English breakfast.

He did not go quietly. He would not have been the man that he was if he not been a fantacist to the end. Taken out into the street he yelled and struggled, persuading passers-by that the two police officers holding him were really criminals and he was being abducted. They leapt to his aid. The police officers came under attack but one, although he had lost his trousers, managed to produce his warrant card. After apologies, they were allowed to take him back to Cambridge and then on to prison in Bedford.

Woodfall came before Mr Justice Streatfield at Norwich Assizes on 14 January 1964. Mr Jack Abdela, prosecuting, said: 'All this stupendous talk of fabulous wealth was a complete facade, a complete sham from beginning to end. This woman was duped, seduced and mesmerised by you.'

In Effie's words: 'He was so very convincing with his lies and that was the amazing part. I didn't think of disbelieving him.'

She spent six hours in the witness box telling the court how it had come about, perhaps comforted to hear that she was far from being the first person to be taken in by him. Stoutly, she endured the ordeal, and faced Woodfall.

When Woodfall gave evidence in his own defence he told what was to be his last tall story. He said it was because of threats by a prison barber to harm Effie and her daughter if he did not obtain money from her that he had done so. He was not believed. How could he be with his record of similar offences going back over twenty-three years!

A medical report on Woodfall said that he was 'a psychopathic personality and a hundred per cent humbug, a firm believer in his own lies'.

There seemed no doubt how the case would end the next day, after Mr Justice Streatfield had made his summing up. Woodfall had already spent many years in one prison or another. There would be yet one more sentence.

But, what Abdela called 'the whole galaxy of pomp, wealth and circumstances' seemed no longer relevant to the man in the dock. In court, he seemed only a shell of the man who had assumed nine names and identities and had once said to a friend: 'You know, old boy, you get respect when you have an important handle to your name, like I have.'

He was taken back to Norwich jail for a last night before the jury, all-male at his request, would be asked to consider its verdict. On several occasions he had talked of suicide. He had once tried it, admittedly half-heartedly. But no chances were to be taken. He was to be treated as a suicide risk.

His cell was stripped almost bare, as he was, but he was allowed a blanket to cover himself. The light was left on in his cell and a check was made on him every fifteen minutes. He covered himself with his blanket, and slept.

The headline of the *Cambridge Evening News* for Friday 17 January 1964 told Woodfall's final story for him, perhaps the only true one in his life, except that he never had been a major:

MAJOR KILLS HIMSELF IN PRISON CELL

Woodfall had managed to hide a minute piece of razor blade somewhere on his person. Beneath the blanket he had made a one inch incision in his left elbow and slowly, unnoticed until it was too late, he had bled to death.

As Effie said when interviewed: 'It was the only way to end it.'

CHAPTER 4

Exhumed at Dawn

1964

What he saw was the half-clad body of his landlady.

Cambridge has long been a city of bedsits and lodgings, streets of the older terraced houses closer to the city centre being given over to multiple occupancy by a fluid population of workers and students at the university. In the 1960s the letting of rooms provided an income that a spinster nearing sixty would have found difficult to come by in any other way, especially one not in the best of health.

Fifty-eight-year-old Miss Cacilie Wollner, a lady from Switzerland, took in four lodgers at her terraced house behind its tiny, walled front garden in Emery Street. It was close to the old maternity hospital and Fenner's Cricket Ground, in the heart of a rambling bedsit area just off Mill Road, a long street

Emery Street, Cambridge. The author

of small shops leading out of Cambridge to the east.

From the summer of 1962 through to December 1963, Miss Wollner had been a patient at Fulbourn Psychiatric Hospital just a few miles from Cambridge, further to the east than Mill Road, where she had been treated for mental health problems. In 1961 she had been considered to be suicidal, but her condition had improved enough for her to need only occasional electrical treatment as an outpatient at the city's Addenbrooke's Hospital by 1964.

Running her little lodging house kept her going and she was on friendly terms with her lodgers. Which was why Domenico Borzillo was concerned when he did not see her after 9 am one morning in mid-July 1964 and did not see her at all the next day. Usually, he saw her at least twice a day. His fellow lodgers had not seen her either.

There was no answer when he knocked on her door on the house's ground floor about 5-30 in the evening of the second day, and there was no sound of movement in the room beyond. What if she was ill? Her bedroom was on the ground floor and Borzillo went out into the small garden to look through the bay of her window. What he saw was the half-clad body of his landlady. She was on her bed with her feet touching the floor. The lower half of her body was naked and her head and her body's upper half were covered by an eiderdown. By 6-30 pm a police constable, M J Law, had entered Miss Wollner's room through the window. He at once notified CID.

Detective Chief Superintendent Joseph Breed, head of Cambridgeshire CID, followed the police constable to 2 Emery Street in response to Borzillo's urgent phone call and the equally urgent reaction of Law, and he was at once very puzzled. How had Cacilie Wollner died? And what had taken place in her room before and at the time of her death?

There was an empty cash box, but there was money in another box. It was open at the bottom of the bed and had a £1 note and a ten shilling note in it. And in a drawer there was nearly £400 in notes. Would a burglar have left that behind? Little seemed disturbed. The room seemed not to have been searched. It was possible that Miss Wollner may have awoken and the burglar had left in a panic in mid-robbery but – the window was closed. Would a burglar leaving in a panic have stopped to close the window behind him?

It was an enigmatic scene and situation. There was just Miss Wollner lying on the bed, half in and half out, arms raised. There were a few small cuts on her right shoulder and on the left side of her neck, as if she had turned away from an attacker. There was a cut on her left hand, as if she had tried to ward off a blow. But none of the injuries was serious and certainly would not have caused death. There was blood on her pillow, but not much. Miss Wollner's face, when the eiderdown was removed, was red and suffused. That was an added complication, indicating that suffocation had most likely played a part in her death. Could it be a case of suicide – by eiderdown?

Breed, initially, did not suspect foul play. Suicide seemed the most likely explanation, especially after her psychiatric problems became known to him. And yet – there were the small injuries, as if caused by a sharp-edged object. And there was no such object in the room.

Dr Austin Gresham, who had become a lecturer in pathology at the University of Cambridge in 1962 and had been appointed Home Office pathologist for Cambridgeshire in the same year, carried out a post-mortem on Miss Wollner's body on 18 July, three days after she was believed to have died. He presented his findings to an inquest on 22 July. It was his opinion that the lacerations on the body had been made shortly before death because they had bled so little, but none was serious and none would have been fatal. A contributory factor in the death was asphyxia, but it was uncertain how big a part it had played. Suicide – or not? And shock – shock was also a possibility. Gresham said that she had not died of natural causes, but he was unable to say exactly how she had died, whether by her own hand or that of another. But there was no clear evidence to point to the involvement of a second person.

Little had been learned from the post-mortem to alter Breed's consideration of suicide. But nothing really pointed to it either. It was a puzzle all right. The uncertainty went on for four weeks and then, on Wednesday 12 August, Breed received a startling phone call from the police in Essex. They had arrested a man who had admitted burglary at Miss Wollner's home in Emery Street, Cambridge, on 15 July. He was speedily brought back to Cambridge to be interviewed by Breed and Detective Inspector F C Lilley.

The man was twenty-one-year-old Rhys Llewelyn Hopkins, a Cambridge hotel worker, who had lodged at Miss Wollner's from January to May of 1964. Hopkins had been spotted by Sergeant D C Series of Essex police sitting in a car in London Road, Newport. When questioned he had said that he was on his way to Cambridge but had run out of petrol. He had then left the car, saying that he was going for petrol. However, Series had noticed some time later that the car was still in the same position and he had questioned its driver again.

Weary and dejected, that had been enough for Hopkins. He had said: 'I'm fed up. Can I talk to you?' He had gone on to say that he had stolen the car in Middlesbrough. Asked if he had committed any other offence, he had said: 'I stole some money from a house in Cambridge. About £100.' The house had been in Emery Street.

Lilley questioned Hopkins first, about the break-in. He admitted going into Miss Wollner's room but was uncertain about whether she had been in the room. Breed then questioned Hopkins about her death. She had been in bed, he said, but he remembered little else. He remembered nothing about an eiderdown. The sash window had been open at the top and he had levered it up at the bottom. Asked if he had had anything in his hand to help him to raise the window, he said: 'I may have had a chisel.'

Hopkins said that he had gone into the room and had sat on a chair while he had shone a torch about 'to see where things were.' He knew that he had been on edge and he thought that he may have lost his temper, but he could not remember the cash boxes. He could not remember taking any money and he could not remember if he had touched Miss Wollner. All that he knew was that he had been sweating and shaking when he had arrived back at his new lodgings and that he had noticed blood clots on his clothing. He had realised then that he must have done something.

Although there were some discrepancies, especially as regards things that he could or could not remember, Hopkins written statement was much the same as his interviews. He began by stating that he had gone out on Wednesday 15 July with the intention of breaking into somewhere. He had taken a torch and chisel with him.

The car that he had been seen driving, or had been seen sitting in at the roadside, had been searched at Saffron Walden police station and a chisel and a torch had been found.

Of his night out in Cambridge Hopkins said: 'I decided I had better hide somewhere and I was near Emery Street. I got into the garden of number two and just sat there waiting for things to quieten down.'

He had then dozed off and had awoken at about 3 am

'wondering what to do'. It was then that he had noticed Miss Wollner's window open at the top and he had decided to get in and see if he could find some money. He had seen some cash boxes in the room and a handful of bank notes and, as he was going to have a further look around, he thought that he may have knocked against something, possibly a bowl of water on the floor. The sound had caused a movement from the bed. He could not remember whether Miss Wollner was in the bed or not:

I heard a noise. I don't know whether she screamed or said something. I must have lost my temper and I cannot remember much after that until after I got back to my digs.

After a restless night, Hopkins had decided to leave Cambridge the next day. He had gone to his home town of Middlesbrough, where he had stolen the car, and then, after spending a night at a boarding house in Saltburn, Yorkshire, he had made his way back to Cambridge, driving the car until it had run out of petrol in Newport.

What Hopkins had told Breed and Lilley and had repeated in his statement was enough to have him charged with burglary, and he appeared before Cambridge Magistrates the next day charged with breaking into and entering the house of the late Cacilie Wollner, and stealing £100 in cash. He was remanded in custody for a week because, as Mr C H Cossham, prosecuting, said: 'There are a number of scientific examinations of an intricate nature which remain to be done.'

But more than scientific investigations were going on. Details had been forwarded to the Director of Public Prosecutions with the result that 'the Director realised that there was a most important decision he must take. In other words in deciding what offences and deciding whether this man should be charged with another and grave offence.'

Sure as Breed and Lilley were that Hopkins was implicated in Miss Wollner's death there was still not proof enough to charge him with that other 'grave offence'. Desperate to get that proof, and feeling that Miss Wollner herself may be able to provide it, they called in the top Home Office pathologist and Professor of Forensic Medicine at London University, Francis E Camps.

The Home Secretary issued an exhumation certificate and, at dawn on Tuesday 8 September, almost two months after her death, Cambridge City Police exhumed Miss Wollner's body at

Cambridge Cemetery where Miss Wollner's body was exhumed. The author

the Cambridge City Cemetery in Newmarket Road for a second post-mortem examination by Camps at Addenbrooke's Hospital.

Camps most celebrated work to date had been the identification of the remains of six women found at the infamous 10 Rillington Place, bringing their murderer, John Reginald Christie, to the hangman in 1953. The death of Miss Wollner may have seemed banal in comparison. But, not popular within his profession because of his arrogant personality, Camps would generously use his expertise in the most undemanding of cases and was never grudging of the time needed to present his findings in court, usually with little financial gain to himself. He would do so in the Wollner case when Hopkins came to trial.

But, despite Camps skill, that second post-mortem on Miss Wollner had resulted in no new evidence to indicate clearly that she had been murdered. Camps' results, on that occasion, were mainly the same as Gresham's. None of her wounds had been made with the intention to cause serious injury. They had been inflicted shortly before death, and the two could have been closely connected, but none would have ended her life. 'They are the sort of wounds inflicted deliberately to cause pain or fear,' he told the court. He concluded that they had been made by a sharp-edged instrument, possibly a chisel, as she had tried to turn from her attacker. The discolouration of the dead woman's face indicated that some form of 'mechanical congestion' had occurred before death to cause either pressure on the neck or pressure over the face. Suffocation had definitely played a part in her death, which had most probably been from shock.

The police still had barely enough to be able to charge Hopkins with capital murder. He still could remember very little of what had happened. All that he seemed sure of was that he had broken into Cacilie Wollner's room. T H Jones, a scientific officer at the Metropolitan Police laboratories, had found it impossible to group the blood on Hopkins' chisel, but found that some on his raincoat had been of Miss Wollner's group B and not of Hopkins own group O. That, the Director of Public Prosecutions decided, would be enough.

Hopkins appeared before Cambridge Magistrates again on Friday 18 September and was then charged with having killed Cacilie Wollner in the course or furtherance of theft. In court he was composed and emotionless, as he had been since his arrest. It was, after all, not his first time in court. As a child he had per- sistently run away from his home in Middlesbrough and he had eventually been sent to a home for maladjusted children. He had run away from there too. It had been diagnosed that he had 'a compulsion to wander'.

He had spent 1961 and part of 1962 in Borstal before being sent back to Borstal again after he had broken into a Middlesbrough shop. He had come to Cambridge in January 1964 and had found lodgings with Miss Wollner.

It was as well that Breed and Lilley had interviewed Hopkins so thoroughly and had taken from him such a complete written statement because, when the case came for trial at Cambridge Assizes in November he said only a few essential words, identifying himself and pleading not guilty to murder, and then he exercised his right not to go into the witness box, a decision which caused the judge, Mr Justice Thesiger, to remark that if a 'certain appearance had been made and they were able to offer an explanation to clarify the matter then one would perhaps expect them to do so'.

As it was, the fate of Rhys Llewelyn Hopkins was to be in the hands of his defence team, led by Mr P O'Connor, and those of three of the best psychiatric brains in Britain. His plea was to be not guilty to murder due to diminished responsibility. The only witnesses to be called on his behalf would be the experts who would testify on Hopkins' impaired mental state.

If the jury was to return a verdict of guilty Hopkins would, under the 1957 Homicide Act, be liable to the death penalty. In

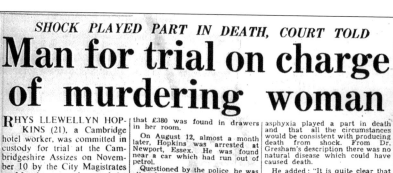

SHOCK PLAYED PART IN DEATH, COURT TOLD

Man for trial on charge of murdering woman

RHYS LLEWELLYN HOPKINS (21), a Cambridge hotel worker, was committed in custody for trial at the Cambridgeshire Assizes on November 10 by the City Magistrates on Monday on a charge of the murder of 58-year-old Cacilie Wollner, of 2 Emery Street, Cambridge, on July 15, in the course of furtherance of theft.

He is also charged with breaking and entering the house and stealing £100 in cash, and with robbing Miss Wollner with violence.

Mr. D. Palmer said that the accused would not give evidence that day or call any witnesses. He reserved his defence.

When the case opened on Friday, Mr. Hugh Cossham, for the Director of Public Prosecutions, told the court that on July 17 Miss Wollner's body was discovered in the bedroom of her house at 2, Emery Street, Cambridge. The body was discovered by one of her four lodgers after she had failed to appear about the house for two days.

The police were called and found Miss Wollner half in and half out of bed, with a thick quilt obscuring part of her body.

An open cash box on the bed below her contained £1 10s.

CUTS ON BODY

"The body was immediately seen to have certain numbers of cuts on it and there was a certain amount of blood about," said Mr. Cossham.

"The first thing the police saw when they looked at the face was that it was extremely red and suffused."

The police were unable at the time to get any indication of the circumstances in which she died, and it was perhaps remarkable that £380 was found in drawers in her room.

On August 12, almost a month later, Hopkins was arrested at Newport, Essex. He was found near a car which had run out of petrol.

Questioned by the police, he was alleged to have admitted stealing the car, and also that he broke into a house in Emery Street, Cambridge, and stole £100.

At Cambridge police station he said that until the previous May he had lodged with Miss Wollner.

"NOT NATURAL CAUSES"

Mr. Cossham said: "The evidence will be that asphyxia played a part in her death, perhaps a substantial part. We are unable to say how substantial, and shock was also the cause.

"We are able to say that death was not due to natural causes."

Mr. Cossham went on: "We are able to say that death was due to asphyxia or shock in greater or smaller proportions, and to nothing else. There is no other cause of death."

He added that the asphyxial element in her death was almost certainly caused by the mattress being over her.

"Whether she died of asphyxia or a combination of asphyxia or shock cannot be proved and is immaterial to the charge at the moment," he said.

"What the prosecution will prove is that she died as a result of what Hopkins did that night."

Witnesses gave evidence that the body of Miss Wollner was exhumed at the Cambridge cemetery.

P.c. M. J. Law said he went to 2, Emery Street at 6.30 p.m. on July 7.

He entered Miss Wollner's room through a window, and found a body lying on the bed with the feet touching the floor. The body was naked from waist to feet.

Mr. Walter Julius Berger, a company director, of 52, Alicia Gardens, Kenton, Harrow, Middlesex, said Miss Wollner was his wife's first cousin and he knew her well. He identified her body on July 18.

Mr. Domenico Borzillo of 17, Fowlers Road, Salisbury, said he previously lodged at 2, Emery Street. He used to see Miss Wollner twice a day, and he last saw her at 9 a.m. on a Wednesday.

At 5.30 p.m. on the following Friday, he saw the landlady's legs through the window and told his fellow lodgers. The police were called and a policeman entered Miss Wollner's room through a window.

POST-MORTEM EXAMINATION

Cambridge University pathologist, Dr. G. A. Gresham, said that on July 18 he performed a post-mortem examination on Miss

asphyxia played a part in death and that all the circumstances would be consistent with producing death from shock. From Dr. Gresham's description there was no natural disease which could have caused death.

He added: "It is quite clear that while the wounds were being inflicted, the woman's right arm must have moved."

RUN OUT OF PETROL

Evidence was also given by Police Sergeant D. C. Series, of Newport, Essex. He said he saw a car in London Road, Newport, on August 12 and Hopkins was sitting in the driver's seat.

Hopkins said he had run out of petrol, that he was the owner of the car and was on his way to Cambridge.

The accused left the car, but later Sgt. Series saw that it was still in the same position.

Witness saw Hopkins again and he said: "I am fed up. Can I talk to you?"

Hopkins admitted that he had stolen the car, and would like to tell him all about it, said Sgt. Series.

Asked if he had committed any other offence, accused said: "I stole some money from a house in Cambridge — about £100."

Sgt. Series said he cautioned the accused, who made a statement. In his statement Hopkins admitted breaking into a house in Emery Street, and taking about £100, which he spent.

He said that on the morning of August 8 he left a boarding house at Saltburn, Yorkshire, and drove around in a car he stole until it ran out of petrol.

Told he would be arrested for breaking into a house at Cambridge and stealing money, and stealing a car from Middlesbrough, Hopkins made no reply.

TWO DAYS BEFORE

When the hearing was resumed on Monday Dr. Kurt Silberstein, the Cambridge police surgeon, said that at about 7.45 p.m. on July 17 he saw the dead woman.

He thought death had occurred about 48 hours before his examination.

Mrs. Johanna Fesenko of 15, Mill Road, Cambridge, said that twice when she went to Miss Wollner's house she saw the accused there —in February and March this year.

Miss Wollner visited her on the evening of July 15, and that was the last time she saw her.

Det.-Sgt. J. Ramsey said that at 2, Emery Street on July 17 he saw the body lying on a bed with both feet to the floor. The head and upper part of the body were covered by a quilt.

Her head was on the bed immediately in front of the pillow and both her arms were upraised. At the bottom of the bed there

Headline: Man for Trial on Charge of Murdering Woman.
Cambridge Independent Press

effect, those experts would be using their professional conclusions in an attempt to save his life. They and O'Connor had to convince the jury that he had been suffering from diminished responsibility at the time that he had allegedly killed Miss Wollner. If they succeeded there would be no death penalty. His life would have been saved.

Whilst Hopkins had been held on remand at HMP Brixton the three psychiatrists had examined him. Dr Donald Webster, a consultant psychiatrist from Middlesbrough who had known him since the age of twelve, knew of a brain injury at the time of his birth and knew of his family's mental health problems, believed him to be suffering from a psychopathic disorder. Dr Phillip Connell, a London psychiatric consultant, had treated him over several years while he had been in charge of paediatric psychiatric welfare at a Newcastle hospital, and Dr T N C Gibbons was a consultant psychiatrist at several London hospitals. All three had spent time with Hopkins while he had been in Brixton and all three agreed that he was suffering from a 'mental abnormality which substantially impaired his mental responsibility'.

A further witness, Dr Calder, Principal Medical Officer at Brixton, however, did not agree with the three experts that the foray into the deceased's room would have put Hopkins under stress and increased his mental impairment. In his opinion, he might even have been perfectly sane at the time.

After the bombardment of psychiatric evidence, it was to be for the jury to decide if, and to what extent, an abnormality of his mind had played a part in Hopkins' actions of 15 July. That decision would be the difference between manslaughter and murder, life and death.

In his closing speech O'Connor reminded the jury that the whole case rested on statements Hopkins had made to the police and that, without them, there was virtually no case against him.

Mr Justice Thesiger, at the end of the trial, made a ninety minute summing up. The 'vital question' was the state of Hopkins' mind at the time of the alleged killing. He seemed to be most unhappy with the plea of 'diminished responsibility' in general, and especially as applied to Hopkins.

Hopkins, he pointed out, had a criminal history going back many years but he had always in the past been treated as 'an ordinary troublesome fellow, and was not put out of circulation because he was substantially irresponsible to the point of being really insane'. He stressed the point that: 'If the word goes around prisons and Borstals that men are easily held to be of diminished responsibility the people who have not got good feeling, who are weak in resisting temptation, may not try to exercise their self-control.'

Perhaps the jury was more swayed by the combined clout of three doctors than that of one judge. They took a little over two hours to return a verdict of guilty of manslaughter on the grounds of diminished responsibility.

But Thesiger was to have the last word when he passed a sentence of life imprisonment: 'In this case it is clear that this person, who had a bad character in the sense that he had broken into and stolen from places and had been committed to Borstals, broke into this lady's house. Because he was of diminished responsibility he failed to control himself. He is therefore a greater danger to the public than someone who has control of himself and does not choose to do so.'

Thesiger went on to say that for a burglar who knocks a householder about, although he does not intend to do them any grievous bodily harm, the sentence that he would usually give would be of twelve to fifteen years. But he did not consider Hopkins to be such a man: 'In this case, I think the accused was and is a very dangerous person to have loose because he helps himself to other people's property by breaking into houses and then this sort of thing happens.' A twelve to fifteen year sentence would mean that Hopkins would be eligible for release after two-thirds of the term were up. Thesiger had concerns about that, as he had had about the effect Hopkins' mental state may or may not have had when he had caused the death of Cacilie Wollner. He concluded: 'I think that the proper sentence to pass is an indeterminate sentence. That will best protect the public providing those responsible for his custody do not consider releasing him until they think it is safe to do so.'

Hopkins had escaped the noose.

A life in exchange for a life.

CHAPTER 5

The Final Whistle

1967

I can't stand little kids getting in my way.

O n the evening of Monday 24 April 1967, Cambridge United played and lost a Southern League match against Romford. The game, in the local press, was said to be have been robust, fast and often exciting, but United had needlessly given away a penalty midway through the first half and had lost. For one young Cambridge United fan it would be the last match he would see from the drear terraces of the Abbey Stadium in Newmarket Road. It would be the last match he would see anywhere.

Eleven-year-old Barry Davison went to the match with his father, a foreman at Cambridge University Press, but he met up with pals, perhaps from his school, Manor School, once he was there.

Abbey Stadium and Coldham's Common. The author

Like many boys of eleven he was a bit full of himself. At half-time he saw a girl that he knew, a sixteen year old waitress, and he teased her, calling her names. Something a sparky little boy might do to any teenage girl anywhere at any time. The difference that night for that boy was that the girl was a psychopath, capable of murder.

Barry lived in Stanesfield Road, across the common, Coldham's Common, which spread between the football ground and the main line out of Cambridge railway station and behind it to Coldham's Lane. The girl lived nearby. They would walk home from the match across the common, going the same way.

Barry saw her again as he left the ground after the match and called her names again, following her. Few sixteen year olds would be happy about a boy hanging about, being a nuisance. There might be an exchange of words. Some might give as good as they got. That girl got angry, and the only thing that she could think of doing was to lay hands on him.

They were beside a shallow brook that meandered through the rough turf and beside the shrub bushes of the common. It still does. The common is much the same today as it was then. She turned and she took hold of him.

Every moment of what had taken place after that, and her reasoning for it, stayed crystal clear in the girl's mind. It would

Coldham's Common. The author

be recounted with a psychopath's lack of emotion in a statement she made to Chief Inspector Christine Willis later that night and through the early hours of the next day as she lay on a makeshift bed in Cambridge police station too awake to want sleep.

Her statement was read when she came before Cambridgeshire Assizes in Cambridge in mid-June and has been recorded by David Thurlow, one of the local journalists present in court: 'I grabbed him and dragged him across the common. He was struggling and shouting. I pushed him into the river (meaning the small brook) and we struggled. He tried to get out but I caught hold of his leg and he pushed me in. He got out and I did, I got my lanyard round his neck and pulled it. I had a knife on my lanyard in a sheath. I said I was going to kill him.

'He started praying. Poor kid, it didn't do him any good, did it? I can't stand little kids getting in my way. I can't understand what all the fuss is about.'

'When I left him his head was in the water but before that he was alive. At least, I think he was. I was leaning over him, wasn't I? His heart was still beating. Well, I couldn't leave him alive, could I? Let's face it. So I shoved his face in the water.'

It was for the other people involved, the families, drawn so suddenly and traumatically into tragedy, to feel the emotion she did not feel, to suffer the horror and the sadness.

After attacking Barry, the girl had gone home and had told her parents that she had just strangled a boy by the brook with the lanyard that she always wore round her neck.

Their reaction was that it could not really have happened. They wanted desperately not to believe her. But she was wet. She had been in the brook. They felt that they had no alternative but to call the police.

The nightmare had begun, for the girl's family and for the Davisons, a family of five.

Police went door-to-door in Barry's neighbourhood while others searched the common. His body was discovered beside the brook about half a mile from his home by a police constable and Terry Thurston, one of Barry's relatives.

The girl appeared at Cambridge Juvenile Court the next day, sitting in silence between two plain-clothes policewomen while Detective Chief Inspector Bernard Hotson, who had led the search for Barry and the house-to-house enquiries, said that he had formally accused her of murder earlier that morning.

Her parents were there to support her and her solicitor, Mr

A new Mini-car—or £500 spend
yours by next week-end. And a
shilling. See Place the Ball entr

BROADMOOR FOR GIRL OF 16

A 16-year-old Cambridge waitress charged with murdering an 11-year-old boy, was "quite clearly mentally ill," Mr. Michael Havers, prosecuting at Cambridgeshire and Isle of Ely Assizes said on Tuesday. The girl was sent to Broadmoor Hospital.

The girl, whose address was not given in court, pleaded not guilty to murdering Barry Davison, of 30 Stanesfield Road, Cambridge. She pleaded guilty to manslaughter and this was accepted by the prosecution.

Mr. Havers said: "This girl after some minor argument with the boy, strangled him and left him with his head lying in a river and he eventually died. She has been examined by several doctors and it is quite clear to them that she is mentally ill."

Dr. Norman Mullin, medical officer at Holloway Prison, who examined the girl, said: "I have come to the conclusion that she is suffering from a psychopathic disorder within the meaning of the Mental Health Act 1959, and I consider she is in need of treatment. In my opinion, it was substantially impairing her mental responsibility and this is the unanimous view of three doctors."

Broadmoor Hospital, he said, were prepared to accept the girl for treatment immediately or within 28 days.

Mr. Justice Glyn-Jones said: "This treatment cannot be given except in a top security hospital and doctors are of the opinion that Broadmoor Hospital is the most suitable for her needs."

Tragic case

Mr. Hugh Griffiths, Q.C., appearing for the girl, said: "This is a tragic case. The girl has been examined on behalf of the defence by an independent doctor and he has come to agreement with the findings of the other doctors. Both the girl and her parents appreciate that she is in need of treatment."

Mr. Justice Glyn-Jones told the girl: "This case needs few words from me. All the medical evidence only leaves one course open to me — that is, to make a hospital order and a restriction order which means that doctors will have to consult the Home Secretary before acting on the conclusion that you can safely be released, if and when you get better.

"There is every hope that you will get better. Broadmoor is a hospital best suited for your treatment and you will go there straight away."

Mr. Justice Glyn-Jones said he had every sympathy for the parents of the boy and he also

Baby girl dies in house fire

A baby girl died in a fire at 35 High Street, Longstanton, on Monday. The baby was Tracey Jane, aged 22 months, daughter of Mr. and Mrs. David Warriner, of 43 High Street, Great Shelford.

She had been put to bed in an upstairs bedroom in the house owned by Mr. and Mrs. H. F. Pennick, who are on holiday in Spain.

The Warriners were visiting the Pennick's grocery store with another couple, Mr. and Mrs. Rowlandson, of 34 Lancaster Road, R.A.F. Oakington.

The Rowlandsons' 19-month-old baby boy, John, was rescued unhurt from a bedroom across the landing. Damage was confined to one bedroom.

Mr. Dennis Pennick said that his sister Pauline had gone upstairs, apparently to collect the baby. "She got as far as the door," said Mr. Pennick. "She shouted that the place was on fire. We could not see a thing, not even the landing."

The baby's father, who heard the shout, went upstairs and grabbed the child from the blazing bed but she was already dead. Bed sheets in flames were thrown through the window by Mr. Pennick and Mr. Warriner.

At the inquest at R.A.F. Oakington on Wednesday doctors said there was "ample evidence" that the baby was alive when she suffered her burns.

Cause of death was given as burns by Mr. M. J. Mitchinson, pathologist, of Addenbrooke's Hospital.

Evidence of identification was given by Mr. Warriner, a sales representative for the Independent Order of Foresters insurance company. The inquest was adjourned pending completion of police inquiries.

Neighbours in street lamp row

A row over a scheme to have one street lamp has split the Cambridgeshire village of Tadlow (pop. 69).

In the centre of the controversy are next-door neighbours Mr. Kenneth Paddock, a 31-year-old aircraft inspector, and Mrs. Marian Hall, a housewife.

At a parish meeting, Mr. Paddock, a Londoner who moved to Tadlow 18 months ago, suggested one lamp at the village bus stop which, he says, would not be a rate burden if it was bought privately.

Then Mrs. Hall got 45 people to sign a petition which made it clear that the majority of the villagers did not want to see a change at Tadlow.

The dispute was summed up in a prepared statement on Monday by the chairman of the parish meeting, Mr. David Sells. The statement read: "The question of street lighting in Tadlow was discussed at a parish meeting some months ago. As a result, it was agreed to study the matter and estimates were obtained from Eastern Electricity for several different schemes.

Circulated

That "women are fickle jades" is well-known and when about 15 of the women of Linton faced 10 of their menfolk on Wednesday night on the football pitch they only enhanced this reputation.

Ex-Celtic and Cambridge United forward, Ian Sharkey, had a hard time keeping order in this fancy dress soccer match which ended, it is thought, in a 3-all draw.

The rules of the Football Association were thrown into the nearby river Granta—along with half the male team. All this may not have been cricket but it did raise more than £16 towards a new village hall to be built soon.

The women's captain was Mrs. Winifred Shillon of The Crown. The fancy dress football was the second event in Linton's festival week. The main event will be a float procession and fete tomorrow.

Restraint by police praised

Police officers were commended at Cambridge Magistrates' Court on Tuesday for using restraint against a rowdy crowd of between 200 and 300 youths on Market Hill, Cambridge, late on Saturday night.

Six youths who appeared in court in connection with the disturbances were told by the presiding magistrate, Mr. E. F. Andrews: "There must not be a repetition of this kind of behaviour in Cambridge on Saturday nights.

"It appears that these disturbances have blown up in recent weeks, and it must stop. The police are to be commended on

Hea
pla

A preview of t to the parish cou practitioners, a d to 10 prams and

The plan is to the Ministry of Health Committee bridgeshire and County Council. county council's mittee will also b
The centre, opposite, the School, would be timber harmonised 10,000 persons at Babraham. Cost ft. building was £40,000.

Litt

A letter to Sou shire Rural Cou that litter collectio whole district, encouraged to use centre," was read
The letter repres step in the debat two councils occ district council Sawston may have clearance bills.
In a letter to th shire and Isle o Council the coun restoration of th sections of which i been ploughed an impassable The from Church Babraham, from B

Headline: Broadmoor for Girl of Sixteen. Cambridge Independent Press

S J Green, sat with them. He said that he could not apply for bail for the girl. It would not have been considered. Earlier in the proceedings he had stood beside her as she had said: 'I have nothing to say at this stage.' She was remanded in custody to come before the Cambridgeshire and Isle of Ely Assizes in about two months time.

As with the case of Rhys Llewelyn Hopkins, accused of murdering Cacilie Wollner three years before, the time between the girl's two court appearances was to be put to good use.

It was obvious that she had acted insanely but it would be in the girl's best interests to have her state of mind professionally assessed. She was examined by several doctors, including Dr Norman Mullin, the medical officer of HMP Holloway, and they would all present their findings when she next appeared in court.

When she made her second court appearance at the Assizes, defended by Hugh Griffiths QC, her plea was one of guilty of manslaughter. It was accepted by the prosecution, led by Michael Havers who had defended Dennis Pratt in his 1956 trial for the murder of Rachel Parsons.

Havers said: 'This girl, after some minor argument with the boy, strangled him and left him with his head lying in a river and he eventually died. She has been examined by several doctors and it is quite clear to them that she is mentally ill.'

Mullin, speaking of his findings, said: 'I have come to the conclusion that she is suffering from a psychopathic disorder within the meaning of the Mental Health Act 1959 and I consider she is in need of treatment. In my opinion, it was substantially impairing her mental responsibility and this is the unanimous view of three doctors.'

He went on to say that Broadmoor Hospital was prepared to accept the girl for treatment immediately.

Unlike the Hopkins case, there was no doubt that the right decision about the girl's mental state and her future had been made. The judge, Mr Justice Glyn-Jones, said: 'This treatment cannot be given except in a top-security hospital and doctors are of the opinion that Broadmoor Hospital is the most suitable for her needs.'

Hugh Griffiths, the girl's defence, could only agree, saying: 'This is a tragic case. The girl has been examined on behalf of the defence by an independent doctor and he has come to agreement with the findings of the other doctors. Both the girl and her parents appreciate that she is in need of treatment.'

The hope, for the girl, was that she would get better with the treatment that she would receive in Broadmoor. She was young enough. There was hope. Mr Justice Glyn-Jones spoke to the girl of that hope, of a future: 'This case needs few words from me. All the medical evidence only leaves one course open to me. That is to make a hospital order and a restriction order, which means that doctors will have to consult the Home Secretary before acting on the conclusion that you can safely be released if and when you are better. There is every hope that you will get better. Broadmoor is a hospital best suited for your treatment and you will go there straight away.

Every hope. A future. But for Barry Davison there could be no future. He had heard his final, final whistle.

CHAPTER 6

When West Brom Won the Cup

1968

The happiness is gone.

On the morning of Saturday 18 May 1968 eight-year-old Christopher Sabey went shopping in Huntingdon with his mother. He was the youngest of the nine children of George and Violet Sabey who kept the *Falcon* public house in the village of Buckden, on the A1 to the west of Cambridge.

When he got home he changed into a grey shirt and long grey trousers with a blue pullover and then went out on the red bicycle he loved.

Described by his father as active and energetic, Christopher, well built and with dark brown hair and eyes, was a friendly lad who enjoyed the company of other children and teenagers.

About 1-15 pm on that Saturday he bought and ate fish and chips for his lunch from the mobile van on the village green, and then he was off again, cycling about the village. But there were few sightings of him. One was by a woman who saw him pedalling by the village shop, Milner's, and along Church Street, going towards his home in Mill Lane, at about 3-15 pm. There was little more.

It was Cup Final day. West Bromwich Albion were playing Everton and the match was being televised. It turned out to be a disappointing match and there had been no score at full-time. It went into extra time and it was then that Jeff Astle, the country's leading goal scorer with thirty-four goals, put the ball into the net for West Brom in the 93rd minute, the only memorable moment in the game.

But it had been enough to keep most of the village's residents off the streets. When she walked down the main street while the match was being televised, Mrs Connie Davies, the vicar's wife, noticed that there was 'literally nobody out of doors'.

But Christopher was out, riding his bike.

When he had not returned home by evening his parents became anxious. He cycled about, but he was never far from home. Becoming increasingly worried, they called the police.

The police were there quickly, a missing child was a top priority, and word soon spread that Christopher could not be found. The police, Christopher's brothers and sisters, and villagers began to scour the streets and surrounding areas where he might be.

An obvious place to look was the old gravel pits at Hoo Farm, about 200 yards from the *Falcon*, described by police officers as a 'paradise playground' for Buckden's youngsters. A search was begun there but because the terrain was so treacherous the police 'quite sensibly' called it off as night closed in while continuing to look all night elsewhere.

At first light the following morning, Christopher's twenty-year-old brother, Keith, went back to the gravel pits with a friend. At 4-15 am they found his body, lying against a grassy bank. An hour later, Dr Daniel Connan of Huntingdon was examining the body in the pits. The cause of death was believed to be asphyxia, resulting from compression of the neck.

The police set up a mobile murder HQ on the village green, opposite the school, where the fish and chip van had stood, and Detective Superintendent Ken Jones of Scotland Yard was called in to lead the investigation into what he called 'the worst possible type of murder'.

While keeping other possibilities in mind, it was treated from the start as a Buckden murder, with Detective Sergeant Reginald Brothers, a colleague of Jones' from Scotland Yard, saying: 'At this time my channel of inquiries is localised'.

Parents were stunned and horrified, guarding their children, escorting them to and from the village school, not letting them out of their sight. One mother said: 'The atmosphere is terrible. It is as if a shadow has come down. Mothers are really frightened.' A father said: 'The happiness is gone.'

And yet the detectives, in the first days after Christopher's body had been found, trying to piece together the boy's last movements, came up against a veil of silence. Up to fifty officers called at houses, posters were put up, and patrol cars broadcast appeals for information, but residents were slow to try to help.

Jones spoke of the silence: 'Villagers at this place are rather secretive and this is why we must drum it into them the importance of coming forward. There is not a lot of information coming in voluntarily. We are having to go out and find it.'

Perhaps the children of the village would be more forthcoming. Parents were urged to question their children to see if any of them knew where Christopher had been between 1-30 and 3-15 pm, between the two sightings of him on his bike, and between 3-15 and 5-00 pm. It was believed that he had died at, or shortly after, 5-00 on the Saturday afternoon.

Detective Inspector George Smith, the head of Huntingdon CID, took a team of detectives into the village school and the 270 children were asked if they had seen Christopher. Enough details were gently drawn out from them for police to be able to have a good idea of the route he had probably taken as he had cycled about the village until, finally, he had left his bike propped against a cement mixer beside a half-built house on a building site at Hoo Close, next to the gravel pits.

One highly relevant sighting emerged. It was the only one which seemed likely to be of crucial significance. While no adult other than the one woman who had seen him heading for home had seen Christopher after the match had kicked off, a six year old boy said, crucially, that he had seen Christopher on a path leading to the pits at about 5 o'clock. He had been with a slim, fair haired youth in blue jeans and a black blazer. Finding that youth became of vital importance.

As the search for the youth intensified, routine enquiries continued and villagers at last began to talk to the police, their reticence fading. A thousand people were interviewed in the first week of enquiries by up to one hundred police officers working from Mid-Anglia Police headquarters at Brampton. Some, on the instructions of the force's chief constable, Frederick Drayton Porter, had been drafted in from other divisions to help in the investigation. Their nightly ration of sleep was five hours and some did a 120 hour week. Day and night at least ten detectives kept a vigil at the heart of the operation, the murder room at Brampton. The lights never went out. But little progress seemed to be made. It was slow going.

They were hard days for the Sabey family. Violet Sabey, behind the bar at the *Falcon*, pleaded: 'Please help in any way you can. You might be able to prevent this great sorrow being brought to another family.'

Jones, who was holding daily news conferences, refused to say exactly how Christopher had died as it 'may affect later evidence', but he did say: 'There is no question of horseplay between two young children,' before adding, tersely: 'It was brutal all right.' Medical examination of the body by a Home Office pathologist had shown that Christopher's killer had pressed his knees so hard onto his shoulders that an imprint of

Frederick Drayton Porter, Chief Constable Mid Anglia Constabulary.
Cambridgeshire Collection

his clothing had been made on the flesh. He had been manually strangled. When his clothing was examined, three dog hairs were found on his pullover. Jones kept all of that information to himself.

The search for the youth seen by the child brought Richard Nilsson, of Shooter's Hollow, Buckden, an eighteen-year-old plasterer's labourer, to the attention of the police. He worked at the building site where Christopher's bike had been found and he fitted the child witness' description.

Interviews continued and 2,500 questionnaires were handed out for completion. Nilsson was amongst those interviewed and of all those interviewed only he 'put up a line of defence composed of lies which, at an early stage, were impenetrable'. He said that he had been at the building site between ten and eleven on the day of the murder. He had been there again about one, having arranged to meet a friend there, but when the friend had not turned up he had gone into Huntingdon on his moped. He had got home about 4-15 pm and had stayed in for the rest of the evening. He had heard of the murder the next morning. He knew Christopher, but he had not seen him 'for weeks'.

On 21 May, Nilsson was interviewed again, and his story of how he had spent the day of the murder was not quite the same. He said that he had gone into Huntingdon on his moped and that he had got home about 4-30. He had last seen Christopher about 1 May. A police officer had then asked him to fill in a questionnaire and he had noticed that Nilsson appeared very nervous and had been sweating, although it was a cold morning. He had also kept swallowing. The way in which some of the answers had been given had struck him as 'being vague'.

With suspicions roused, the police subjected Nilsson to further interviews during which he offered varying accounts of his movements. While they were still going on, Christopher's funeral took place. It was held at St Mary's, the fifteenth-century village church where he had attended Sunday school, ten days after his murder, with 150 mourners cramming into the pews to hear the vicar, Reverend Enoch Davies, say: 'Never have the residents of Buckden got together in such tragic circumstances and never have we felt ourselves so inadequate to meet such a tragedy. In the untimely and cruel death of young Christopher the village has been silenced and I am sure no words of mine can express our feelings.'

In bright sunlight, his coffin was taken to the nearby churchyard, detectives mingling with the mourners and staying after the service to list the names on the hundred wreaths.

During his interview on 4 June Nilsson said that he got home from Huntingdon between 4-30 and 4-45 pm. 'I turned on the television – it was ITV. The match was on but I didn't notice what stage the game had reached'. He said that at 5-05 his mother had said that she wanted him to go to the shops for her, but he had refused 'because I didn't fancy going all that way again'. He had gone outside, had taken a wheel off his moped, and had gone back into the house. He quite often spent a lot of time working on his moped. His blue moped was his most prized possession – apart from his golden Labrador dog. He added, quite definitely, that he had never seen Christopher at the building site.

On 13 June, over three weeks after the murder, Nilsson was asked to clear up some 'discrepancies' in his previous interviews, and it was then, at last, that he played into Jones' hands. In a desperate bid to clear himself once and for all he said: 'If I did it my fingerprints would have been on Christopher's neck, wouldn't they?'

That was the moment Jones' astuteness in not disclosing exactly how the boy had been killed had been leading up to. Jones pounced. Asked how he knew that Christopher had been manually strangled, Nilsson said that it was 'the talk of the village'. A lie too far.

In custody, he had been interviewed again later the same day and the matter of the three dog hairs on Christopher's pullover had been raised. He was told that they matched those of his dog. He had said, at once: 'Anyone can get dog hairs on them. The milkman calls at our house, and the dustman.'

He had then been asked yet again about his movements on the day of the murder. He had admitted then that he had lied before. But this was the truth. This time he was telling the truth. He had seen Christopher that day, at about 1-45 pm. They had swept up in a house under construction, part of Nilsson's job as a plasterer's assistant, and they had talked about darts, about a match at the *Falcon* that Christopher had been allowed to win by his brother and Nilsson. Then he had gone. He had left him there.

Asked why he had lied before, and on more than one occasion, Nilsson had grinned and said: 'I always lie to save my neck.' Asked if he meant that, he had said: 'Yes, if it will get me out of trouble.' And why had he said that he had not seen Christopher Sabey? 'Because I was scared. I thought I would have been the last to see him alive and you would have thought

I had killed him.'

But that was still not the end of Nilsson's attempts at deception or, as he was alleged to have told a girl, of leading the police 'up the garden path'. On 17 July, a police officer went to Nilsson's cell and was at once told: 'What I said before was a lot of lies.' He was ready to make yet another statement. In that one, he said that Christopher had followed him to the building site. They had swept up and had talked about the darts match. After about 45 minutes he had left him there and had gone home. That had been at 5-15 pm. He had got home at 5-30 and the match had still been on.'

That was his final statement, and probably the nearest that he ever got to telling the truth.

A crowd of more than 150 lined the street outside St Neots Magistrates' Court on Thursday 18 July, two months after Christopher's death, when Nilsson appeared to be accused of his murder.

Nilsson's trial was held at Nottingham Assizes early in December. His plea was one of not guilty and his defence, Mr B Wigoder QC, asked for acquittal. The evidence against him was 'slender indeed' that he had committed what was, by any standards, 'a beastly, horrible, nasty and motiveless murder'.

Nilsson did not go into the witness box because, said Wigoder: 'He is a young man of nineteen of no great intellectual capabilities. He would have created the most dismal picture before you of a wretched youth not knowing which way to turn, not knowing how to get out of one difficulty after another into which his lies had led him.' There would have been a very real danger that the jury would have approached their verdict with the feeling, "We don't think much of you." That sort of consideration has no part to play in this case.'

Nilsson did, however, make a twenty-six word statement from the dock. He said: 'I had nothing to do with Christopher Sabey. I did not kill him. I had nothing to do with his death in any way at all.'

By the time that the case came to court the police had taken 4,600 statements in what, at the time, was the biggest manhunt ever undertaken by police in the Cambridge area.

The fact that 18 May had been Cup Final day and the match had been televised had enabled police to take decisions about the various time factors involved in the case. So many statements, including Nilsson's own, had made references to 'the match' that Alec Weeks, the producer of the BBC coverage, was called to give evidence of timing. He told the court that kick-off had been at fifty seconds after 3-00 pm, and that the match had ended at 5-24 pm.

When the prosecution case, presented by Victor Durand, began, Nilsson's adored golden Labrador, Susan, was brought into the court. Damningly, the three hairs found on Christopher's pullover and presented as evidence had been scientifically proved to tally with hers. Other matching hairs had been found on Nilsson's jacket and jeans. It was claimed that, as he had knelt on Christopher's shoulders, Susan's hairs had been transferred from his jeans to Christopher's pullover.

Villager Mrs Connie Harris then told the jury, as damningly as the dog hairs, that at about 4-25 pm on the day of the murder she had looked through her window and had seen a boy on a bike following a man on a moped. The boy had been about five feet behind and the moped rider had slowed and allowed the cyclist to catch up before they had disappeared from sight in the direction of the building site.

Mrs Harris said that a blue moped, produced in evidence in court, was the same as the one that she had seen that afternoon. It was Nilsson's moped. Of the moped rider Mrs Harris had seen, Durand claimed, "It was the accused who, shortly after 4-30, was in School Lane, followed by Christopher, whose life was to be ended within the next three quarters of an hour.'

Nilsson was a well-known figure about the village, riding his moped 'jockey fashion.' His moped, too, his pride and joy, was well known. It was a distinctive colour and model and, unfortunately for him, it was the only one of its type in the area. Durand said: 'He and the moped were one – it was his alter ego.'

The jury was out for two and a half hours before returning a guilty verdict.

The judge, Mr Justice Blain, said: 'There was no semblance of provocation. You have been found guilty of the murder of an eight year old boy and the statutory sentence is one of life imprisonment. I see no reason to say anything more.'

The two things closest to Nilsson's heart – his golden Labrador, Susan, and his blue moped – had betrayed him.

CHAPTER 7

Up at Cambridge

1970

*The sharp splintering of glass and the bass rumble
of riot had been heard, spreading across the city,
and far beyond . . .*

With its earliest college, Peterhouse, founded in 1280, and sharing with Oxford University a reputation as the foremost academic institution in Britain and one of the most respected in the world, the University of Cambridge has always been a forum for political thought, discussion and the open expression of opinion.

To be 'up at Cambridge' has long been thought proof of academic excellence. It has prepared for a career in politics and government countless members of parliaments, cabinet ministers and prime ministers of this country and others. In the late 1960s the heir to the British throne was up, at Trinity.

At that time, along with those at other universities at home and abroad, Cambridge students needed little encouragement to take their political views onto the streets in demonstrations. It was their right in a democratic society and in keeping with all the traditions of western universities. Meetings, sit-downs and marches were held, banners and placards were flourished, voices were loud and posters and graffiti appeared on Cambridge walls. But there was little real disorder in Cambridge when similar demonstrations at other universities, such as Paris and Tokyo and our own Warwick, were becoming violent. But that was about to change.

In November 1967 there had been a far-left fracas around the Guildhall in the Market Square during which visiting prime minister Harold Wilson had been jostled and jeered. Only belatedly, after criticism, had two students been arrested for their part, and the university had taken no action. A spokesman had said that it would be wrong to blame undergraduate organisers for it not having been the peaceful demonstration they had planned.

Just a few months later, in March 1968, foreign secretary

Denis Healey had been beset by hundreds of students in an even wilder demonstration than the one that Wilson had faced. The view of a university spokesman then had been: 'You cannot run-in all members of the university who happen to be on the highway.' The students had not broken any university rule. No action would be taken despite concerns for the peace of the city and the safety of its residents, expressed by civic leaders. A councillor said: 'This continued excuse by the university authorities doesn't work with ordinary people like myself.'

But after those high-profile confrontations and criticisms one university man, DGT Williams, a fellow of Emmanuel, decided that if student demonstrations were not to be curbed he should, at least, point out the pitfalls to participants. In *Notes for the Guidance of Members of the University and Others in Demonstrations in the Streets* he set out the legal position and warned those involved of the offences that might be committed and the penalties that could follow. He recommended that the police should be told of demonstration plans at an early stage and that there should be liaison with the university's own 'policemen', the Proctors, and their assistants, the Bulldogs.

It worked. Police believed that it was Williams' paper that had kept Cambridge demonstrations non-violent from 1968 through to 1970. But, despite that, the more extreme or militant left elements at the university were itching to become confrontational. They wanted attention, on an international scale if possible, and for them shouting through a megaphone was not enough. They wanted more.

The flashpoint came in February 1970, when it was decided to hold a Greek Week in Cambridge, to promote tourism. To most people it was just one more attempt to sell holidays abroad. There had been several before where people had picked up brochures and a few may have been persuaded to go on a holiday to wherever it was.

But as far as certain students and their political groups were concerned Greece was different. Greece was a beautiful, sunny country. It had glorious islands. It had history. It had Athens. But, in 1970, it also had a fascist military government. The military had come to power in 1967 after a coup which had forced the king to flee the country. It was Greece's forty-ninth government in fourteen years.

Backed and encouraged by the Cambridge Greek Appeal Committee, notice was given three or four days before Greek Week began that there were to be demonstrations against it planned by a broad cross-section of Cambridge undergraduate political groups. The week was felt to be more about politics than holidaymaking It was a political stunt financed by a Greek government which had chosen Cambridge to popularise the regime and make it seem acceptable amongst academics.

The *Shilling Paper*, founded in 1968 by left-wing undergraduates to be a voice for the radical left in the Cambridge student movement, did its best to stir things. In its edition of 6 February, under a headline of 'The Show That Will Make You VOMIT,' it made it clear that a demonstration was being planned at the world-renowned *Garden House Hotel*, beside the Cam, on the evening that a gourmet Greek dinner and dance was to be held. A warning to the hotel's management appeared in the same issue. It should order the police to be there as, 'YOU WILL NEED THEM.' The paper's readers were told to 'WATCH THIS SPACE NEXT WEEK FOR DETAILS OF YOUR ROLE IN THE EVENING'S ENTERTAINMENTS.'

In the meantime, the letter 'Z', for free Greece, was to be painted and sprayed on as many prominent Cambridge walls as possible. It was. Detective Superintendent Bernard Hotson of the Mid-Anglia Constabulary said: 'Many of these signs now

Garden House Hotel, *terrace and gardens.* Cambridgeshire Collection

associated with the Greek Week will remain for years as evidence of the talents of the vandals who used aerosol sprays.'

The police knew that some demonstrations were being planned for Greek Week and that the Garden House dinner was to be a target, but that was all that they knew. Any meetings held in college or university buildings were classed as private and were closed to the public and to the police. They had to collect what bits of information they could where they could and hope that the plans they made were the right ones for dealing with whatever might arise. Williams' wise words were forgotten. They were no more.

On Friday 13 February, the day of the dinner, the front page of the *Shilling* urged all its readers to be at the *Garden House Hotel* at 7-30. The centre pages, in an article headed 'Cambridge Evening News SHIT,' accused the local press of exaggerating demonstrations that had taken place during the week when they had not amounted to much more than 'stink bombs'.

Cambridge police at that time were hard-pressed by a series of arson attacks, and one did take place during the evening of the dinner, but as many officers as could be made available were on duty at the *Garden House* on a dark and very bitterly cold night. The hotel, at the end of a cul-de-sac, had attractive gardens to the rear, by the riverside, and a car park to the side. As recommended by the police, it had brought forward the time of the pre-dinner reception to avoid whatever trouble there might be as guests arrived. The university Proctors, in cap and gown, and their Bulldogs were to be on duty, just in case.

At first there was an orderly build-up of students with placards in the cul-de-sac, but soon a minority wanted more action than placard waving. They jostled late-coming guests in their evening dress and tried to stop them entering the hotel. Police helped some to make their way through to shouts of 'Shame' and 'Fascists'. They were called pimps and prostitutes.

A public address system had been set up from nearby college rooms for supporters of the Greek people to speak to the crowd but, disappointingly, it did not work.

The number of students grew – there would be more than 500 – and the space in front of the hotel became packed with demonstrators, press reporters and photographers and the police. Some students showed their athleticism by climbing onto the hotel roof and a wall. Then a call came for the demonstrators to go to the back of the hotel, beside the Cam, where there were no police.

It was then that 'mob hysteria' had begun to take over as hundreds of students had surged to the back of the hotel to the sound of breaking windows. The sharp splintering of glass and the bass rumble of riot had been heard, spreading across the city and far beyond it, in the night stillness of the Cam and the Backs.

There was a charge on the hotel. Its managing director, Michael Reynolds, who later said: 'A lot of us must have a basic sympathy with the cause of the demonstration tonight. But the demonstrators have done more harm than good,' turned a hosepipe on them from an upper window to try to stop them getting in through the doors. But the water was not enough and stones were hurled at him. The hose had been left, limp, hanging from the window, while some of the demonstrators began to enter the hotel.

Others broke the floodlighting and uprooted the ornamental lamps, some of which were thrown into the river at the side of the garden. The electricity fused. Total darkness. Cloaked in a cold obscurity the mob moved, chanted and threw missiles while shadowy figures at the back of the crowd used a loud hailer to encourage more noise and more disorder. The public address system began to work, blasting out Greek music to add to the general uproar.

The police and Proctors were hopelessly outnumbered. They made no impression on the students who were, by then, beyond reason or control. A Proctor, Dr Charles Goodhart, was hit by a brick, two policemen were injured, and the head of the Cambridge City Police, Chief Superintendent Ronald Barlow, was manhandled, injured and thrown down into a hedge. Police dogs were brought in to try to contain the prancing, chanting pack in the murky, trampled gardens. Cars were being damaged in the car park.

Outnumbered as they were, the police concentrated on the safety of the hotel's guests and staff. They let damage to the hotel go unchecked. It was all that they could do with the manpower available. Forming a cordon they drew their truncheons for the first time in years, leading to a *Cambridge Evening News* comment that while each officer faced the prospect of being killed or maimed he could only defend himself with a lump of wood. Still, they were effective. A number of demonstrators were floored and, wounded in battle, were carried away by their associates while police helmets flew or were kicked about.

But the police had more to contend with than bricks, stones, clods of earth, paint and fists. Much more seriously, there were 'mole killers', light green cardboard tubes packed with chemicals. They were also known as 'stick bombs'. After being lit they produced flames, smoke and sulphur dioxide gas. They were dangerous and could be lethal. Some fell, certainly not as intended, amongst the demonstrators themselves, adding a new urgency to their prancing. One reached the hotel.

Inside the hotel's riverside terrace dining room guests had moved away from the windows as the carpet became one of crystal. Tables and their pot plants were overturned, crockery was broken and chairs were thrown, but as police managed to rid the dining room of demonstrators staff and guests were determined that the dinner should go ahead. It would take more than a student demonstration to stop it.

Stoically, guests ate their way around the glass on their food and ignored the firecrackers, the police, the mayhem still going on in the lounge and the riot raging outside. Lighted squibs thrown in were calmly extinguished by the restaurant manager, Charles Taylor, with a soda siphon as the waitresses continued

Garden House Hotel *and the River Cam.* Cambridgeshire Collection

serving and the guests continued eating and drinking. The guests later congratulated the waitresses and took up a collection for them. Service far beyond the call of duty.

At about 11pm the demonstrators decided to go to the *Royal Cambridge Hotel*, about half a mile away along Trumpington Street, where a similar dinner was being held. They marched there in the centre of the road, disrupting traffic, and then, when they found a cordon of police preventing further bedlam, they marched back and disbanded in the Market Square.

Of the more than 500 involved, nine students were arrested and three of those were discharged. Six appeared before city magistrates charged variously with wilful damage, obstructing and assaulting police and carrying an offensive weapon. There was outrage. The Mayor of Cambridge called for a tightening of university discipline and a clampdown on political extremism. He called for penalties. What had happened to good old gating? And sending down?

The MP for Cambridge, David Lane, said: 'Cannot the violent demonstrators realise that they are behaving like the

Royal Cambridge Hotel. The author

fascists they detest who smashed the windows of the Jews. Academic freedom is precious and must be defended, but this freedom will turn sour if it is no longer blended with a measure of discipline and order.'

A statement by the Cambridge Socialist Society hailed the riot a success and said that they had no sympathy with the hotel owner for the considerable damage caused, adding: 'The affair is nothing to do with the university.' The general manager and director of the *Garden House* and *Royal Cambridge Hotels*, Mr K Morton Chance, thought otherwise. The university authorities would be pressed for some compensation. 'I have no doubt that we shall be writing to the Vice-Chancellor about this because, although our broken windows may be covered by insurance I very much doubt whether the ruined gardens are.' And the Chief Constable of the Mid-Anglia Constabulary, Frederick Drayton Porter, was forming his own views. He said: 'Having looked carefully into the various reports I am of the opinion that what occurred that night amounted to a riot. Arising from this about twenty undergraduates may appear in court on riot charges with a view to them being committed to Quarter Sessions for trial.' If only they had heeded Williams!

Fifteen students were charged and held in Wormwood Scrubs. After a seven day trial at Hertfordshire Assizes at the end of June, shortly after Prince Charles had received his degree and had left Trinity, eight were found guilty of rioting and Mr Justice Melford Stevenson imposed prison sentences on them ranging from nine to eighteen months. Two other students were sent to Borstal, one of them the grandson of the artist Augustus John. Seven were acquitted. One was recommended for deportation to Brazil. Predictably, none of them were the shadowy figures at the back of the crowd. They had remained free, free to orchestrate another demonstration on another day.

After the sentencings, about forty students held a vigil outside the Guildhall for their imprisoned colleagues, handed out leaflets and gathered signatures for a petition for their release. But one old man amongst the crowd of 200 or so onlookers would certainly not have signed. He came armed with eggs, soft tomatoes and flour which he threw at the protestors, decorating the students and creating a technicolour fresco over the walls and windows of the Guildhall.

There was no official reaction to the consequences of the riot from senior members of the university. Asked whether the university would take further action against the convicted students the Senior Proctor, Paul Fairest, said that it was 'far too early' to say. But some dons were concerned – at the severity of the sentences.

Soon after, more than a thousand students marched through Cambridge behind a 'Z' Greek Freedom banner during a Free Greek Rally. Police were on standby, ready for any trouble, but there was no incident. The marchers halted at the police station to hand in a list of more than three hundred names of students who admitted having been at the *Garden House* riot and who should also share responsibility.

They then went on peacefully to Parker's Piece to hear a message from the Greek singer and activist, Melina Mercouri, but the tape recorder did not work. The anarchists amongst the marchers played football instead.

Route of peaceful Free Greek rally past the police station to Parker's Piece.
The author

CHAPTER 8

A Danger to Women

1974–75

I came to rob but I'll stay to rape

On the evening of Friday 18 October 1974, twenty-year-old Frances 'A' was alone in a shared bedsit in a house in Springfield Road. Near Cambridge's Mitcham's Corner, it was in an out-of-the-way spot which could have been reached by a narrow alley from Milton Road. She had enjoyed a leisurely bath and then put on a dressing gown to relax on her bed, reading. The light went out. That sometimes happened in the house. She went to the door and opened it and there, looking at her, was a man with shoulder-length hair.

He grabbed her and, as she started to scream, he clamped a

First rape, Springfield Road. The author

hand tightly over her mouth. As they struggled the girl's dressing gown fell open enough for the man to see that she was naked beneath it and she heard the horrifying words: 'I came to rob – but I'll stay to rape.' Forcing her onto one of the beds, talking constant filth, he raped her at knife point. But he did not forget his original intention. He stole some money before he left the bedsit. Shocked and distressed, the girl dressed and managed to drive her car across Cambridge to tell a friend. Her friend called the police.

An investigation began at once, but, from what the girl told them, the police considered the rape to have been an opportunistic offence by a burglar, a one-off. They would not have believed then that the man who was to terrorise the women of Cambridge through the winter months of 1974 and the spring and early summer of 1975, and hold the city to siege had committed his first rape of seven. In that time the Cambridge Rapist, or the Beast of Bedsit Land as he was also known, became the most notorious and most sought criminal in Britain and Europe.

Within days, while the police investigation into that first rape was being hampered by the lack of useful forensic evidence, largely because the rape had taken place on the bed of another girl who had entertained at least three men, the rapist struck again.

On 1 November, a second twenty-year-old, Anne 'B', was raped in Abbey Road, a short street sloping gently down to the River Cam, down river of the Backs, where Banham's boatyard was situated, the colleges had their boathouses and the eights rowed.

There were similarities. Could there be a connection? What of the one-off? The police felt the chill of uncertainty. Could they be as sure as they had been two weeks before? It was a Friday night again. The girl was alone in her bedsit and she was getting out of the bath when the light went out. A man came into the bathroom and she was threatened with a knife to persuade her not to scream. She was gagged and her hands were tied behind her back before she was carried into the bedroom and raped. Her breasts were badly bitten.

The first victim had said that the rapist was young, in his twenties, was about five foot four inches tall, had long hair and was casually dressed. The second girl said that he was about five foot seven and had long hair. In a darkened room it was difficult to tell more. It was amazing that in the circumstances they

Second rape, Abbey Road. The author

remembered anything at all.

Had the same man struck twice? The head of the Cambridgeshire CID was Detective Chief Superintendent Charles Naan. He and his second in command, Detective Superintendent Bernard Hotson, based at the force's Parkside headquarters in Cambridge, found enough similarities for them to scrap their 'isolated incident' theory of the first rape. There had now been two similar rapes, and a sickening belief began to grow that there would be a third.

A special rape squad was set up and the most probable area for a third attack, where girls were most likely to be alone in bedsits or flats, were put under surveillance by plain-clothes officers on Friday nights. They lay in wait in doorways and shadows.

There was an attempt at a third rape ten days after the second, and it was in one of the areas being policed, but, as if the rapist knew of the police operation, it was on a Monday evening. The rapist made his next call at an annexe at the back of and cut off from a three storey house in Huntingdon Road.

It could not be seen from the main road and it was visible only from Westfield Lane, where the rapist had probably watched, waiting for the right time to strike.

He confronted the girl, Elizabeth 'C', on her doorstep, long-haired, and naked but for a blanket over his shoulders. But, on that occasion, he met his match. The girl struggled with him, even though he used his knife on her, and in the struggle his long hair came off. It was a wig. Beneath it was what the girl and the police believed to be a second wig because his hair was still long. She fought so strongly that he was forced to leave without completing his attack and, horrified, she threw the wig after him. It was gone by the time the police arrived. What would certainly have been vital evidence had been lost.

The rapist moved away from the heavily policed bedsit areas to commit his fourth attack and his third rape. If the police had still had any lingering doubts that a serial rapist was stalking the young women of Cambridge they went with that third rape.

On 13 November he went to Homerton College in Hills Road, a mile or so from the city centre on the way to Addenbrooke's Hospital, isolated in its own grounds. It was a Wednesday. An eighteen-year-old music student, Janet 'D', was practising her cello in a soundproof room at about 8-30 in the evening when the light went out. As she went to see why she was grabbed from behind and a curtain was wrapped around her head to muffle her screams.

Each attack had been more vicious than the one before. Previous victims had been threatened with a knife and slashed with it, and had been bitten about the breasts and abdomen. That one was to be different. At Homerton he pulled the screaming girl into the college grounds where he gave her a savage beating. She was then taken to a remote wooden shed where she was assaulted. That, too, was different. Perhaps because it was the time of her monthly period he committed buggery before disappearing into the night.

The girl managed to reach the main college buildings where two fellow students helped her to the porter's lodge where the police were called. The special squad was quickly on the scene. Aided by dogs and uniformed officers they searched the grounds but found only a dirty, wine coloured silk scarf. It was brandished by the police but the publicity brought no useful response. It was unlikely to have had anything to do with the rapist.

Police statements followed. Detective Chief Inspector Keith Hookham pleaded: 'We are following a lot of lines but we ask the public for any information at all they might have about these attacks.' Naan had words of his own. He had served for many years with the Manchester City force, policing the roughest streets and the darkest back alleys, and he had been involved with the Moors Murders investigation. Announcing that after the severity of the most recent attack the entire police operation was to be stepped up and that extra detectives were to be brought in from the Regional Crime Squad, he said: 'These officers will be engaged on nothing else but these inquiries. This man must be found and we will be making a determined effort to this end.' He also issued advice to the city's many single girls in bedsits or student accommodation. 'Young women should make sure that doors and windows are securely locked and bolted when they are at home on their own. Anyone whose suspicions are aroused in the slightest should immediately call the police.'

In the local press there was another police statement, no doubt meant to build confidence. Perhaps the police's own, knowing that they faced and must be equal to an enormous challenge. They had a one hundred per cent record in solving rape cases and were sure that they would keep that record. But they must have realised after that Homerton attack that they were up against a master of his art and, at that time, the inquiry that they were carrying out had no precedent in the annals of British crime. Homerton had put it in a niche all its own.

From previous rapes and the doorstep attack police had a rough idea of the man they were seeking and a photofit and wanted posters, the first of many, had been put out. He was a long-haired, casually dressed, slim, not very tall, young man. After the Homerton rape they had a new chilling description to circulate, the one that would come to personify the Cambridge Rapist. For the first time he had been dressed entirely in black leather. Most terrifyingly of all, black leather had even encased his head. He had worn a helmet-style hood with eye slits and a mouth fitted with a heavy duty 'shark's teeth' zip which he had opened and closed as he had talked threat and dirt. Naan had stated the obvious. He must be found. Quickly.

The girl soon returned to her studies at Homerton, but the memory of that hood must, surely, have lasted much longer than her bruises. By a quirk of coincidence that third rape victim was the sister of the rapist's first victim in Springfield Road, Frances 'A'. A Warwickshire family, proud to have two daughters at the University of Cambridge, must have suffered with them. The worry to every family with a girl alone in the city must have been almost unbearable.

The serial rapist stalking the young women of the university city of Cambridge was, by then, of nationwide media interest. It made all the national newspapers, sensationalised in some. With the rising interest came the questions, putting pressure on the police. Naan could talk of his force's one hundred per cent record – but this rapist had not been caught. Why? What were the police doing? Were they up to the job? Should they call in help from other forces? In response Naan and Hotson invited the people of Cambridge and the media to visit the incident room at Parkside to see for themselves what was being done. They were invited to come up with better ideas. Any would be welcome. There were none. It could be seen that the investigation was well in hand and the criticism faded, temporarily, leaving the three hundred officers, on shifts of one hundred, to continue working up to twenty hours in every twenty-four.

The plain-clothes officers of CID were constantly on the case. Uniformed men volunteered for overtime week after week with not one man putting in a claim for extra pay. All leave was cancelled. As the inquiry progressed 40,000 man hours would be spent on it, 10,000 bedsits in a seven and a half square mile area would be policed, 15,000 phone calls handled, 30,000 pieces of information dealt with and 3,482 statements taken. Every available officer in Cambridgeshire was mobilised, even the 'top brass', the divisional commanders, in the force's biggest ever operation to catch any single criminal. The cost was staggering.

Night after night, officers in plain clothes were put on the streets of the bedsit areas equipped with night binoculars. They were told to stay in one place as inconspicuously as possible. They must listen for screams.

The rapist, a man of the night, must have known what was going on. It was a predictable police response. Perhaps it was his challenge. He seemed to treat it as though it was when, on 8 December, a twenty-one-year-old student, Elizabeth 'E', was asleep in the early hours of the morning in her room in a block of flats in Owlstone Road, Newnham. She was awoken by a sound at her door. She opened it, and there was the rapist. She knew at once who her late visitor was because the leather hood now had the word RAPIST above the eyes in large white letters. He said it saved the introductions. He had got into the building through the back door. He held a knife to her throat and took her out into the back garden where she was raped.

After that rape Hotson said: 'We are looking for an extremely sick and dangerous man. We believe he is highly intelligent but with a completely split personality. The man may well commit these vicious attacks then return home behaving completely normally. He is a man with a vicious streak and a sick mind. We want him badly but our inquiries are hampered by the fact that he always operates in darkness and without any set pattern.'

The rapist's next victim, a week later, was a twenty-year-old Scots-born telephonist, Shelley 'F', who returned to her flat late at night. In some ways it was a revenge attack because it took place at the flat in Huntingdon Road where Elizabeth 'C' had put up such a fight on her doorstep that he had been forced to flee. She no longer lived there. At 4-30 in the morning, on that occasion wearing a wig and a false beard, the rapist met with a new but equally feisty girl. She later gave an account of what took place. It was typical of his first two attacks except that she was more seriously stabbed and had to spend weeks in Addenbrooke's Hospital:

> *I was awakened by a torch shining in my face, then I felt the knife at my throat. I began lifting my head from the pillow and felt the point. I was wide awake. I thought Oh, my God! I remembered the girl who had the flat before and all the stuff in the papers. I knew what was going to happen. I kept asking how he got in. He didn't say anything for a long time, and then he said, "I can break in anywhere." His voice was low and husky. I was fighting and I got out of bed and got to the light. He was startled and I couldn't believe what I was seeing. It was just not human. He was about my height – five foot four. He had a mass of hair, dark, like a wig, and this beard covering most of his face. He banged the light off and tried to pull me towards the kitchen. But I fought again. With the light going on I had seen all the blood on the pillow and the top of the bed. I thought then it was no use and I gave up fighting.*
>
> *He pushed me onto the bed and tied my hands behind my back. Then he cut my nightdress from the hem to the neck. He did not tie my ankles or gag me. He tried but I wouldn't open my mouth so he put the quilt over my face. I kept asking: 'Why are you doing this to me, why are you doing it?' After a while he said: "I don't know".*

She was left bound and bleeding on her bed, cut on her face, hands and arms. She managed to free herself and stagger to the front of the house and bang on a window. Her concern then was for her neighbour, for the alarm of the awakening, and for the shock she would cause.

The neighbour later said: 'I opened my door and she collapsed on the floor covered in blood. I knew what had happened. I had a premonition about it and I had warned the girls here that he would be back.'

A warning that had gone unheeded.

After that rape, detectives came up with a suggestion, shocking in the mid-1970s, that girls should have their boyfriends or a male friend spend the night in their bedsit. Predictably, the idea, when the press got hold of it, caused outrage. It would encourage promiscuity. But some girls welcomed the suggestion. And it did work and saved several girls from attack. One girl told police that the rapist had come to her room, had seen a man there and had said: 'Sorry mate – wrong room,' and had left. All that the police with dogs had found on that occasion were lingering traces of ether.

After that fifth rape, on 15 December, there was a four month gap. There was a belief in the press that the man may have gone away. 'The siege of Cambridge may be over.' People began to breathe more easily. The police, however, knew differently. They said nothing, keen not to let the rapist know that they were keeping close tabs on him. But they knew that in that gap, between mid-December of 1974 and mid-April of 1975, he had visited at least fifteen bedsits. At some he had scrawled a cryptic lipstick message on a window – 'Sleep tight – the Rapist.' Sometimes, more sinisterly, the message had been on a mirror inside.

Going on the descriptions given by the girls, detectives interviewed and saliva tested 1,644 men in the Cambridge area who were in their twenties and under five foot eight. Of those, a hundred had a criminal record.

As early as December, after the fifth rape, police officers and others who knew of his criminal past had begun putting a name forward: Peter Samuel Cook. He was the right size but he did not seem the most likely prospect. For a start, he was in his forties, twenty years older than the man they were looking for. He was a burglar and housebreaker par excellence who, in the early 1950s, had been responsible for a one-man crime wave in the city. But he had never used violence or committed any sexual offence. There was no legal reason to make him undergo a saliva or blood test. He was on file, but no more. And he was, after all, 'going straight'.

Cook had been born in Cambridge on 17 August 1928 and had been raised in the area of the city around Springfield Road and Abbey Road, the scenes of the first two rapes. His was an ordinary, decent family. His father, Sam, was a builder and plasterer running his own business and respected by all for his fairness and honesty. He and his wife, Dora, were good, loving parents. That love had been put to the test time and again over the years but it had remained constant. He was their son.

Peter had been only nine when he had first come to the notice of the police for stealing, although at an even younger age he had set fire to his father's shed and had attacked other children. From then on the police were rarely out of his life as he went from the courts to approved schools and a nautical training school, where attempts were made to save him from a criminal future.

He did not want to be saved. He already had one conviction for housebreaking when he was called up to do his National Service. He joined the Royal Artillery but was discharged, for undisclosed reasons, after fifteen months.

Between prison sentences Cook worked as a bricklayer and designer. He helped to build Cambridge's Bradwell's Court of shops, flats and offices, demolished in 2006, and also worked on the Lion Yard complex of shops in the city centre. When working as a scaffolder he was known as The Human Fly for his fearlessness in walking along narrow poles between buildings, and he was also called The Weasel because of his sharp and shifty looks. But his heart lay in his real occupation. Crime. And he was good at it, calling himself Black Diamond or Black Ace. He might even send a telegram to the commander of the Cambridge CID, Joe Breed, telling him where his next burglary was to be. He would be in and out despite a police watch, elusive as a flea.

He once threatened to kill Breed and his wife, a threat bravely ignored by both of them. They knew him too well. He was a villain, but harmless. And there was a good side to him, shown when he visited Breed in his final illness, taking him a bottle of sherry. Cook sat on his bed and, like old friends, they chatted over past times.

On occasion Cook was arrested – even the best are – and the problem then was keeping him. It became his boast that he could break in or out of anywhere. In 1952, in court in the Shire

Hall in Cambridge for shop breaking, sentenced to five years and awaiting transport to Dartmoor, he got out through a manhole cover over nine feet up in the ceiling by standing on the shoulders of another man. Small and powerful, he pulled two other men out after him. While on the run he sent a letter to the *Cambridge Evening News*, published on 20 January 1952, detailing his exploits while he had been free. Pride before a fall. He had been recaptured soon after.

Belatedly in Dartmoor, he was given the job of bricking up a wall and, for Cook, doing porridge came to mean just that. According to a fellow inmate, as he bricked up he set a three foot square area with porridge and pointed it off with cement. Undetectable. His way out was there if he wanted it.

Years of thievery followed in the late 1950s and 1960s. A favourite hiding place for stolen goods was in the River Cam. But he worked far beyond Cambridge. He made the continent his own, stealing in France, Spain, Switzerland, Belgium and Austria before being deported from Germany. In Britain he was known to have stolen in Plymouth, Stratford, Oxford, Derby, Manchester and Glasgow, serving sentences when caught and escaping when he could.

After a spate of burglaries on commercial premises in Cambridge in 1965 he, for some unfathomable reason, managed to talk himself into the Broadmoor mental institution. He stayed there until 1968 although, later, the authorities admitted that he had never belonged there. He was quite sane.

He was still under Broadmoor supervision when, on 3 August 1968, he married twenty-six-year-old Margaret Rose Dickerson at St Mary's, Comberton. Perhaps with reason, her family was not thrilled. Cook's was. It could be his salvation. His parents' hope was that he would 'settle down' as a married man.

His father had bought some land cheaply in Hardwick which he had later sold for building at a considerable profit. He gave his son £12,500 as an incentive, hopefully, to keep out of trouble. And it seemed to work. He got a steady job as a delivery driver with Dolamore's, a Cambridge wine firm, and he stuck to it. He was pleasant, well liked and reliable as he took deliveries to colleges and around the city.

His parents lived in a bungalow which Sam had built to his son's design. Cook and his wife lived next door in a luxury mobile home which he had named Villa del Sol after the favourite Spanish hideout he went to when wanted by the police.

With his father's money Cook bought a Land Rover and a boat, which he named *Margaret Rose*, after his wife. He could use the boat, moored at Upware, to take his wife for nice days out. And he did. Always down river towards Ely. But it was a four-berth, ocean going cabin cruiser fitted with all navigational aids and equipment, including a deep-sea echo sounder for serious sailing on the high seas. It was designed for far more than a gentle chug along the Cam, for something more like a quick getaway abroad. Perhaps to the other Villa del Sol. Porridge in Dartmoor. A cabin cruiser on the Cam. Cook always liked to have a way out.

Four months of no rapes and then on Sunday 13 April 1975 there was a sixth rape in Marshall Road, just across Hills Road from Homerton College where the rapist had claimed his third victim five months before.

The twenty-three-year-old, Gail 'G', was spending her first weekend alone in the ground floor bedsit that she shared with three other girls. The flat was secured and her bedroom door was bolted. When the rapist broke in through a back window in the early hours he forced the bolt. The sound of the bolt being

Site of former Banham's Boatyard, now redeveloped. The author

wrenched free woke the girl. The door opened and, for the first time, the rapist chose to put the light on.

Police believed that his new disguise with its skin-tight leather hood, difficult to dislodge, made him feel secure enough to risk the light. He was in his full gear of hood, now with white paint around the eyes and false hair around its lower edge, and black leather jerkin, trousers and gloves.

He threatened the girl with a knife, made her remove her nightdress, and then bound her with clothing he found in the room and raped her. He bound her so securely that she was unable to move for six hours after the rape and it was about 9 am before she managed to get to a window. When she saw a neighbour walking his dog she gripped a perfume bottle in her teeth and banged on the glass. A surprise for man and dog. The man got in through the bedroom window, untied her and called the police.

Hotson, as the special squad questioned but learned nothing from the girls' neighbours, was by then wishing that he was in a different job. He was the front man fielding renewed criticism and a loud demand that the mighty Yard should be brought in. His view was that the Yard had no more experience of handling a serial rape case than his men had, and his men had the advantage of being on their own patch. All he said was: 'There is no magical method of wrapping this up. It is simply back to the hard slog of routine enquiries. We need the information from the public – because there is no doubt somebody knows this man.' If they did, they did not tell the police.

During the night of Sunday 4 May the rapist, wearing his now notorious black leather gear, made three unsuccessful attempts to get at girls asleep in an isolated New Hall hostel, off Madingley Road. He was defeated by the girls' security measures. All interior doors downstairs had been bolted. In trying to smash open a back door he had awakened one of the girls who alerted the others. They were in time to see him running away through the grounds.

Police found that he had broken a small lattice window in the front door but then had come up against a firm inner door which he had been unable to force. Outside, he had tried a window before smashing the glass in the back door to reach the Yale lock, only to find himself in a locked and bolted kitchen. He had fled when the lights had gone on.

What the rapist had not known was that a male student had been sleeping in a separate part of the house. Another of the girls'

safety precautions. He found that the rapist had cut the telephone wire and he had then had to run to a nearby house to call the police. By the time they arrived he was, of course, long gone.

Although the rapist later admitted to two 'visits' on 4 May in a list of twenty-six that he prepared for the police the New Hall hostel was not included, and neither was his first call at the Huntingdon Road flat when he had been ousted from the doorstep. Perhaps he preferred to forget his failures. A matter of pride.

Just two days later, 6 May, there was again something disturbingly new. For the first time the rapist struck during the day. At lunchtime. And it was a bloody attack. Amanda 'H', a secretary in her early twenties, returning from London, went home to her flat in a house in Pye Terrace, on the opposite side of the Cam from Abbey Road, at lunchtime. It was something that she had never done before.

As workers at the nearby Pye electrical works went by along Church Street, the rapist, who had let himself in through the front door with a duplicate key and had already been in the house, waiting, when she had arrived home, cut off her clothes, tied her with tights and raped her, stabbing her viciously in the stomach. After the attack she had managed to stagger to a phone box in Chesterton Road and had called an ambulance. The ambulancemen had called the police. She was taken to Addenbrooke's for an emergency abdominal operation while police swooped on the area.

Road blocks were set up. Cars were stopped. As were all men around five foot five inches in height. They were questioned and searched. A report was received of a long-haired man with a bottle tan and sunglasses cycling by. The description was rushed out. But had he anything to do with anything? It would never be made clear. Hotson said of the girl's attacker: 'This man was small, wearing a brown zip-up anorak and the inevitable black leather hood.' No hood was found on any man stopped. No one was detained. The rapist, with his slippery skill, had got away again.

Unknown to the latest victim, because she had been away, the Pye Terrace flat that she shared with two other girls had been broken into the previous day. The other girls were actually at Parkside reporting the incident when their flatmate was raped. The rapist, with his usual cunning, had broken in and familiarised himself with the flat before the rape which had then taken place exactly where and when he had planned. As officers downstairs in Parkside were being told about the break-in, in the rape incident room upstairs a call came in to report the rape at the same house.

Only later, as they returned home and saw the police there, did they learn what had happened. And one of the girls, also a secretary, realised that she had had a lucky escape. Usually she was the one who went home for lunch, and would have done so but for having to report the break-in, and the girl who had gone home on that day usually never did.

The daytime attack gave the police the opportunity they had been hoping for to check up on the movements of their main suspects. Peter Cook was one of them, but he had proved impossible to get anything on. He had given a new meaning to the word 'clean'.

After the 15 December rape he had been invited to Parkside for a chat with detectives working on the case. He had arrived with a copy of the photofit of the rapist, the 'Wanted' poster displayed on the door of Dolamore's, where he worked, and in the *Cambridge Evening News* office opposite in Newmarket Road, where he went every day to pick up a paper and chat to the girls about the latest rape. Cockily, he had pointed out that he was almost forty-seven, twenty years older than every victim had claimed the rapist to be. He denied everything. And what could the police do? They had no reason to hold him or to make him undergo any tests. Short Cambridge men between the ages of seventeen and thirty had been given saliva tests, and so had the many men in Newmarket of the age and size. But Lester Piggott had missed out because he was too tall and a few other top jockeys had been too old. The police had tried to trick Cook into giving a saliva sample, but he had been too crafty to be tricked. He knew that without evidence against him the police were powerless.

They dogged him all the same. The roads to and from Hardwick were watched at night, but there was no sign of him coming or going. After almost forty years he could suss a plain-clothes officer, even in the dark. His caravan was searched, but it was clean. His home was always clean. Over the years he had never kept anything incriminating where it could be connected to him. If nothing was found he was in the clear. The search had been repeated in February with the same result and a member of his family had alibied him for the times of the rapes. That had seemed to be that. Until the daytime rape. Work alibis could be checked.

Squads of police raced to the workplaces of all the main suspects. Cook was at work in Newmarket Road, just across the

Marshall Road, across Hills Road from Homerton College. The author

Cam from Pye Terrace, when police reached him, busily loading his delivery van. He said that he had been at Banham's at the time of the rape. To boost his income he sometimes used his Land Rover and a trailer to transport boats across country for the Cambridge boatyard. It was a matter of yards from Pye Terrace, moments away via the towpath. Cook could easily have slipped away and returned, unnoticed in the bustling yard. But three people at Banham's, one of them a senior executive of the firm, confirmed that he had been there.

Naan, asked later why police had not brought Cook in at that stage, said that there had been another stronger suspect of the age and height of the rapist and with connections in the areas where girls had been raped. He said: 'It is easy to be wise after the event. Despite the rumour and gossip all we had against Cook was his height. You cannot prosecute or even arrest on rumour. We were dealing with a cold, callous, cunning, clever criminal who knew he was safe while we had nothing on him.'

The three who had alibied him at Banham's had to be believed. They were reputable men.

They were positive that Cook had been there at the time of the rape and the police had to accept that. So, the search went on while the audacity of the daytime rape brought a new crop of responses. While flowers were being taken to the stabbed and raped girl in Addenbrooke's, police made a Do You Know Your Neighbour? appeal. Hotson said: 'It is not a case of spying. It is a case of getting to know who your neighbour is and what he looks like so that any stranger will be immediately noticeable.' A free bodyguard service for girls was set up by students at Gonville and Caius. It could be arranged for two male students, ones not known to each other, to stay overnight in a girl's flat. It proved to be a welcome service. But police warned against the vigilante patrols being set up in some areas. Hotson said: 'We are not involved with a ninety minute Western.' The *Cambridge Evening News* offered a £1,000 reward for information leading to an arrest and two local businessmen bolstered that to £1,500. Meanwhile, the city's MP, David Lane, got involved, making a television appeal to the rapist's mother. She was to stop shielding him and go to the police. There were lots of people getting involved, there was a lot of well meaning action, but it was all to no effect. Except, perhaps, that it put people more than ever on their guard. Everyone everywhere watched and listened and waited.

Owlestone Croft. Cambridgeshire Collection

Selwyn Road where the Cambridge Rapist was arrested. Cambridgeshire Collection

Selwyn Road in 2007. The author

Four weeks after the Pye Terrace rape, in the wee small hours of a still, sultry June morning, not everyone was asleep in Owlstone Croft in Newnham, a hostel for staff at Addenbrooke's. Jane Sproul, a Canadian medical clerk, was saying goodnight to her boyfriend. Following police advice, she had let him stay later than usual. Downstairs, Everall Ballantyne, a senior porter at the hospital, was in bed but not asleep. Just beyond the rambling building, Barry Jeffries and Ray Holland were enjoying some night fishing in the Cam, catching eels.

In nearby Selwyn Road, a short and narrow residential street, terraced on one side and with houses and gardens on the other, Michael Lawrence was up, tending his sick wife, while outside, in the street's shadows, between a hedge and an alley, Terry Edwards, a detective constable in plain-clothes, was spending yet one more night watching, listening and waiting.

As he did so, the Cambridge Rapist was already inside Owlstone Croft. He had already selected Jane Sproul as his target and had waited for her boyfriend to leave. When she heard a sound at the door she thought he had come back. But no.

When the rapist attacked her, slashing her arms with his knife, her blood spurting over the door and walls of her room, she screamed. She screamed so long and loud that the rapist ran. As he ran through the hostel's corridors Everall Ballantyne, Barry Jeffries and Ray Holland all knew what those screams must mean.

When Ballantyne found other girls with the victim in her blood splattered room he went to dial 999. The fishermen headed for Owlstone Croft but, unlike the rapist, they could not get in. The door was chained. Holland ran to a phone box. Jeffries said: 'I could see through the glass of the door and I saw this bloke flash down the corridor – hood and all.' The police were at once on their way to Owlstone Croft.

Detective Constable Edwards remained at his post, as told. He had also been told to stop everyone. He saw a bike without lights racing towards him: 'I stayed as was my instructions until it came to me. Then I stepped out and shone my torch into the rider's face and said Stop! Police! The rider made to swerve past me and I grabbed him by the shoulders. Then I saw the long blonde hair and thought God, I've clobbered a woman. Then in the struggle the wig came off and I saw a face I remembered although at the time I couldn't put a name to it. I was surprised by his strength. He fought like hell and I tried to keep him close to me because I knew he had a knife. He struggled free and ran down the road. I grabbed him again and we both crashed over another cycle and then into a parked car. He rolled half under the car and I grabbed his arm and rammed my foot into his shoulder and then he couldn't move.'

Michael Lawrence ran out of his house, its lights shining on 'two blokes fighting'. On Edwards instructions, he searched the rapist and took his knife from him. With his radio broken in the fight Edwards could not call in to say that he had made an arrest. It would be a little while before he would learn that he had caught the Cambridge Rapist. He and the four other people involved in the arrest would later share the reward money. His well earned £300 would go to the police benevolent fund.

The man, dressed as a woman, was Peter Samuel Cook. His cunning and knowledge of the law had kept him safe from arrest for eight months. His bedtime reading had, after all, been a hefty volume on police law. With that same knowledge he knew that, with his rapist's gear found in his possession, the game was up. Immediately, he admitted his guilt in the hope that it would count in his favour when he went to court. But he knew that he was heading for life imprisonment.

In two plastic bags on the handlebars of his bike when Edwards had knocked him from it were a home-made black leather hood with a zipper mouth (he had used an old shopping bag to make it), various blonde wigs, a rubber torch and spare batteries, pink toilet paper, two watches, one with a strap and one without, a tin box containing tobacco and cigarette papers, a sheath knife on a cord, a shaped and sharpened nine inch bread knife, an ether pad and ether, four pairs of women's tights, two jemmies, tights knotted and plaited into a rope, black leather gloves, a bunch of skeleton keys, wirecutters, a hairbrush stolen from an earlier victim, a length of rubber pipe with an attachment for fusing lights, women's dresses, shoes, underwear and make up, and a pair of trainers. The police had needed evidence against him. That should do.

And that was only the start. Six hundred items were found under the floorboards of his workshop behind his home, where he had spent many hours, and more were found hidden about the two and a half acres around it. The caravan was, of course, clean, as was the boat when they came to search it.

Among the items found was a hard-backed notebook, Cook's own directory of girls, listing countless names and addresses, phone and key numbers, even what newspaper each girl read. It became clear that he had visited every street in the city's bedsit and hostel areas and had a key for most doors in them. Each key was tagged and listed. His record keeping was meticulous. His knowledge of all the streets and all the back alleys in Cambridge was encyclopaedic. In his own crime world he could be called a 'mastermind.'

There was pornographic material too, the inspiration for him to turn what he had read and seen from sexual fantasy into his own sexual reality. And there was his passport and a supply of foreign currency, ready for a quick getaway, perhaps in the *Margaret Rose*.

In all, police took away twenty-five large plastic sacks of items and fifteen large brown exhibit bags.

Cook came before Mr Justice Melford Stevenson at Norwich Crown Court at the beginning of October 1975. He pleaded guilty to six rapes, one buggery and two cases of unlawful wounding. It was all that he could do. And the guilty plea spared his victims having to appear in court. One girl, brought by police from her home in the Midlands, was there to see him sentenced.

Melford Stevenson said: 'I would not be doing my duty if I did not impose upon you for each of the counts of rape life imprisonment and, in the context of this case, life will mean life.' With a flourish of his hand he told Cook's jailors, one at each side of him, 'Take him away.' He went back to Leicester, where he had been held, and then on to the high-security Parkhurst in the Isle of Wight.

His wife swore to stand by him but for his father, Sam, the loving had ended at last. In an interview he said: 'If I had known, had any idea, I would have killed him. Maybe it is a hard thing for a father to say about his son but I really would have done it. I am shattered. I am now a broken man.'

Dora, Cook's mother, or, as Sam called her, 'my poor old girl', took to her bed. He said it had nearly killed her.

Eight years into his life sentence came the final twist in the story of the man who is Peter Samuel Cook. Before his arrest he had stunned two women who worked in the kitchen of the small *Bird in Hand* public house across Newmarket Road from his workplace and almost next door to the *Cambridge Evening News* office. Cook usually had lunch there, often in the kitchen. One day he told them that he had nearly been a woman. When they did not believe him he pulled up his shirt to show them two operation scars where he had had breasts removed.

He could have been telling them the truth. In 1960 he had

Bird in Hand *public house*. The author

gone into Addenbrooke's to be tested for Klinefelder's Syndrome, the symptoms of which are small testes and a small phallus, absence or near absence of sperm resulting in infertility, and female-like breasts. If what he had told the women was the truth he may have come to wish that he not had his breasts removed because, in September 1983, a Sunday newspaper reported that he had made application to the Home Office for a sex-change operation. He wanted to be a woman. Unofficial sources said that it was unlikely that permission would be granted. It was thought to be a ploy by Cook to get into a hospital that he thought he would be able to escape from. It was said that he was calling himself Janet.

CHAPTER 9

Turf War

1975

*Willie Carson was dragged from his mount and
beaten about the legs with his own whip.*

The headline on the front of the *Cambridge Evening News* on Saturday 3 May 1975, 'BULLDOZER RAMPAGE AT RACECOURSE', stunned the horseracing world. The first editions were on the streets about noon. At 1-30 racing was due to start on the centuries-old turf of the Rowley Mile at Newmarket and at 2-15 the most important race on the third and last day of the Spring Meeting, the Two Thousand Guineas, was due to be run. But would it be?

In the early hours of that Saturday vandals had stolen a bulldozer from a nearby building site and had used it to gouge

Welcome to the Rowley Mile. The author

fifteen three foot deep holes in the racecourse. They had then driven it down a mile length of the course, uprooting marker posts and severing race timing and telephone wires. Driverless, it had then been left to crash through a fence and plough across the lawn of the Silver Ring.

While greenkeepers worked all-out to try to repair the damage so that racing could go ahead as planned, the Clerk of the Course, Nick Lees, said: 'Whoever did this was hell bent on stopping racing here today and making a lot of people lose a lot of money. I am bitterly, bitterly angry. It is the action of totally irresponsible fools.'

The 'irresponsible fools' were believed to be Newmarket stablelads who were on strike for more pay and better working conditions, perhaps aided and abetted by troublemaking trade union heavies from elsewhere, drawn by the dispute.

Through the early 1970s relations had been strained between stablelads and the trainers who employed them. Some were unionised, and there was a Transport and General Workers Union representative in every one of the town's thirty racing yards, but many of the younger men in racing had chosen not to be in a union. They were the militant minority who, in February 1970, began a go-it-alone strike for more pay and leisure time. It was designed to prevent the start of the new flat racing season. On that occasion, after marches through the town and demonstrations at the gallops on Warren Hill, the strike had fizzled out and the season had begun without a hitch at Doncaster in mid-March.

In a repeat of 1970, trouble had flared again over wages and conditions in the opening weeks of the 1975 season. By then, more lads were in the TGWU, although Newmarket was still the only racing centre in Britain to be unionised.

The town's 570 lads exercised up to 1,000 thoroughbreds on Newmarket heath each morning for a basic weekly wage, without overtime, of £23-50. They wanted more. Their employers, through the Newmarket Trainers' Federation, said that they could not afford to pay them the extra £4-47 they were demanding. The future for racing, it was said, was 'very, very dicey' and if owners were asked to pay more they would take their horses somewhere else to be trained and lads would have to be laid off. The most that they could offer was £3. It was not enough. There was deadlock.

As the Guineas approached, the first classic races of the season and the most important races in the Newmarket calendar in which the country's best three-year-olds would run, the TGWU called its members out on strike. Two hundred lads answered the call.

It was a time of strikes. Gas, car and railway workers were out and, in Newmarket, there was unrest amongst domestics at the hospital and the printers of the local newspaper, the *Newmarket Journal*. The unions were calling the shots and, in that atmosphere, they brought their clout and their flying pickets to Newmarket – and all for £1-47 a week.

On Thursday 1 May, the first day of the Spring Meeting when the fillies race, the One Thousand Guineas, would be run, picketing of the town's stables began at dawn and pickets were also out at the Rowley Mile and the nearby stabling area, The Links. As the horseboxes began to arrive some drivers refused to cross the picket lines. Horses were unloaded before the line and walked across.

Lads staging a sit-down on the road to the racecourse allowed cars by, but coaches were stopped. Many of their drivers were members of the TGWU and would not have passed them anyway. Racegoers had to leave their coaches and

The road to the Rowley Mile. The author

walk the last half mile to the course.

At the racecourse, catering and bar services were hit, as was the photo finish. Some Tote officials refused to work. But the most serious outcome was that television technicians blacked out 'racing from Newmarket', disappointing the many armchair punters in their own homes.

Trouble began just before the first race when about seventy lads staged a sit-down on the course and held up the start for fifteen minutes until moved by police. Then 150 lads staged a second sit-down, and a third. But worse was to come. Banner and coat waving lads tried to stop the runners in the 2-30 going down to the start.

Willie Carson was dragged from his mount and beaten about the legs with his own whip. The remaining jockeys, led by Frankie Durr, lined up cavalry-style and charged their way through. Some were stopped and their riders pulled from the saddle. Hundreds of infuriated spectators, who had been cheering the jockeys on, then jumped over the rails to tackle the lads, urged on by a remounted Willie Carson.

In scenes unparalleled in the history of racing, angry lads, owners, jockeys, trainers, bookies and punters met and fought on the track with police trying to control the pandemonium. More than a few black eyes were handed out. Later, in court, it was described as a case of 'whips, shooting sticks, thoroughbred horses and people with a grievance one against the other'. If only the TV cameramen had not been out in support! What footage! But the race did eventually start, twenty-five minutes late.

The runners in the later One Thousand Guineas were taken over the heath to the start instead of down the course and the lads, perhaps licking their wounds, did not intervene.

Only twenty-five police officers had been on duty that first day, although one of them had been the assistant chief constable for Cambridgeshire. Newmarket straddles the boundary of two counties and for the second day 200 more were brought in from both the Suffolk and Cambridgeshire forces. Mounted police from the Metropolitan Police joined them.

Despite the serious disturbance that had taken place at the course and the prospect of more to come the chairman of the Newmarket Trainers Federation, John Winter, said that there would be no increase to their pay offer. One of the sixteen union shop stewards orchestrating the mayhem at the course said: 'The lads were asked to go on the course yesterday. They will certainly do the same today if asked. This time they could well

Newmarket Journal

Incorporating the Newmarket Free Press, Cambridgeshire and Suffolk General Advertiser.

Thursday, May, 1, 1975

No. 4703 Est. 1872

(5p)

Stablelads strike but...

GUINEAS TO GO AHEAD

threat
down
alty

down the accident and at Newmarket General an angry response from local townspeople.

Already the Jockey Club and a local councillor are planning to again take up the fight with the Suffolk Area Health Authority.

It is the second time within 12 months that the health authorities have talked of the possibility of closing down the wing.

After protests from the Jockey Club, individuals and Forest Heath District Council last May, nothing more was heard of threats to close the wing — until this week.

One reason to "review" the accident and emergency department is that the consultant orthopaedic surgeon who has run it for many years is about to retire.

The area health authority also points out that comprehensive accident centres are now at nearby Cambridge and Bury St. Edmunds and that Newmarket by-pass is about to be opened.

Costly

"The authority has before it a wide range of options from full continuation of the service, through various categories of partial service to complete closure," said a spokesman.

"To maintain a 24-hour-a-day seven-day-a-week service would be costly and would require the recruitment of a new consultant and supporting staff, he pointed out.

At the other extreme there were problems of providing enough ambulances to convey casualties speedily to Cambridge or Bury — "though this may be facilitated by the new by-pass."

No decision is to be taken until all interested parties have been consulted.

Forest Heath councillor Alan Chapman told the Journal: "The reasons given for closing down the department are nonsense. We shall have another go to keep the casualty wing as it is.

Jockey Club agent Mr. Robert Fellowes said that closure would be a retrograde step and should be resisted. In the past, the casualty department had provided a most valuable and important service to the racing industry.

Tempus...

does...

fugit...

"That clock certainly had a wild time at the weekend.

As fast as photographer Peter Faulkes could click his shutter three times, Newmarket's Rookery timepiece had advanced one hour.

Earlier this week, the hands came to a halt at 9.20 — and there they stayed. So, for once, it was telling the right time twice a day.

About the only time the clock has ever been right was when radio personality Terry Wogan performed the unveiling

Picketing stablelads are out to stop Newmarket horses reaching the Rowley Mile racecourse for the start of the three-day Guineas meeting this afternoon.

The lads took up their positions at the course, The Links gallops and the stables straight after a strike meeting yesterday morning, attended by nearly 200 lads.

Horse box drivers are among those who have agreed not to cross any picket lines, said Mr. Sam Horncastle, district secretary of the lads' union.

Support for his members pledged by other unions would hit food and drink suppliers to the course and put the photo-finish apparatus out of action.

Any intimidation could result in horses from outside Newmarket being stopped, added Mr. Horncastle, but he made clear the dispute was only with local trainers.

The Jockey Club at a special meeting on Tuesday made secret contingency plans to counter any disruption during racing.

Threatened

Picketing began early yesterday morning outside Bruce Hobbs' Palace Houses stables. He had threatened to evict stablelads from his premises claimed Mr. Horncastle.

But along with other trainers, the Palace House horses appeared to have been exercised as usual. Mr. Hobbs was able to use the large paddock behind his yard.

At Henry Cecil's Hamilton Road stables, 15 lads out of 38 failed to turn up, but among those remaining coped. John Oxley said that his staff were all working as normal: "I really haven't been affected by the strike at all," he said.

"I have seen pickets lines on Fordham and Bury roads,

and down at Rowley Mile. They were shouting abuse, but were generally quiet, and didn't upset the horses."

Trainers' Federation chairman John Winter may call a meeting this week to see if any of his members need voluntary help.

"Everybody is working hard to keep the animals happy. Some members may be harder hit than others, and we will see if they need additional voluntary help.

Bitterness

Twenty-six-year-old Tom Tench, a shop steward at Harry Thomson Jones' yard, said that using labour off the streets was breaking the security laws of racing.

He warned that continued use of street labour would only increase bitterness when striking stablelads saw strangers riding out.

Most of this labour was unsuitable for riding out, and if the strike continued, the horses would suffer because of lack of exercise.

Outside yesterday's meeting, one young stablelad spoke of how his trainer boss had taken back the suit and jodhpur boots given when the lad began work.

The trainer's wife told him, he said, that he would never get another racing job in Newmarket.

He was leaving on the next train home to Guernsey. A fellow stablelad had already gone home to Scotland.

● The lads are asking trainers for £4.70 a week rise on their basic wage of £23.50. The trainers have agreed to pay an extra £3 a week back-dated to March 17.

Headline report from the Newmarket Journal, *1 May 1975. Newmarket Journal*

stay on the course for longer than they did yesterday.'

But torrential rain put paid to that. The day became more one of respite, of gathering strength for the third day, the big day, Two Thousand Guineas Day.

Racing would definitely go ahead despite the overnight joyride with the bulldozer. The colts classic would be run – unless the striking lads had other ideas.

About eighty lads went onto the track just before the Two Thousand Guineas, sat down by the three furlong post and held a meeting. When the twenty-four runners were already in the starting stalls more lads sat down in front of them. About a hundred others, singing and shouting, ran onto the course from both sides to a roar of disapproval from the crowd in the stands.

They charged about, dodging the police, on foot and mounted, who were trying to catch them and head them off. There was chaos and, in the middle of it, one eighteen year old got more than he expected. He was chased round the course by his mother trying to stop him taking part in the demonstration, but he insisted, 'I'm striking for more pay just like everybody else.'

Lads who sat down were bodily removed and bundled into three waiting black marias. Fifty were taken away. But strikers were still on the track when the race was run. The stalls had been surrounded, lads jeering at jockeys, scuffling with police and chanting: 'We don't want the Guineas.' Officials were forced to resort to the good old method of starting. They had put the runners in front of the stalls and started the race with a flag.

Angry boos from the lads greeted the 33-1 winner, the Italian horse Bolkonski, trained in Newmarket by Henry Cecil and ridden by Gianfranco Dettori, Frankie's father. The favourite, the wonder horse Grundy, was beaten into second place.

After the race an attempt was made to cool the situation. The strikers were to be allowed to march down the course surrounded by a tight cordon of police and then they were to quietly disperse. They marched, chairing Tommy Dickie, the lad who 'did' Bolkonski and would lose his share of the prize money because he was one of the strikers. They carried him over their heads, waving and singing, and then they could be seen going away across the heath.

Fourteen stablelads were charged with threatening behaviour likely to cause a breach of the peace in a 'vulgar, old-fashioned brawl.' On Tuesday 6 May thirteen lads – a juvenile had been excluded – appeared before Newmarket Magistrates and they were each fined £20, almost a week's wages. They all admitted the charge and all, said Sam Horncastle, the tough district secretary of the TGWU and one of the instigators of all that had taken place, would have to pay their own fine. The union did not condone law breaking.

The lads of Newmarket had made a new kind of racing history. The violent events of the Guineas meeting left them badly shaken. But not the trainers. They stuck to their £3 offer. They had the whip hand, and knew it. The lads were told to tear up their union cards or their job would be gone and, in many cases, their accommodation with it. Several, disillusioned, left Newmarket and racing for good. Some were forced back to work. The militants, supported by postmen, dustmen and the National Union of Seamen, continued to strike and to demand arbitration. After picketing race meetings throughout the country they marched down the course at Royal Ascot and a letter was passed to the Queen. They could do no more and could go no further.

The trainers, at last, agreed to arbitration. On 24 July both sides met and a deal was worked out to give the lads a decent living wage: £37. With the help of Lord Oaksey and ex-footballer Jimmy Hill, lads unhappy with the role of the TGWU in the dispute formed their own association, which trainers were invited to join – the National Joint Council for Stable Staff.

The split world of racing could begin to heal, but no one would forget the turf war of '75.

Newmarket High Street. The author

CHAPTER 10

Booty

1976

Safe breaking was a speciality . . .

On Tuesday 9 November 1976 seven men, all living in Cambridge, came before Judge David Wild in Cambridge Crown Court charged that between 3 January 1975 and 2 July 1976 they conspired together and with others to commit burglary. They were also charged with conspiring together and with others to handle stolen goods. In total, they faced twenty-eight charges relating to fifteen burglaries. They all pleaded not guilty to all of them.

So many and so various were the charges against each man and against all seven of them that their trial was to become a test of the mental powers of prosecution, defence and judge, but, most of all, of the members of the jury. They would be required to bring in more than fifty verdicts.

The Guildhall and Market Square. Cambridgeshire Collection

Judge Wild advised that they should look at each charge against each man separately and then decide one way or the other. But they must also consider the most crucial issue: 'Throughout the case keep at the back of your mind the charge of conspiracy. Keep it at the back of your minds all the time at every stage of the evidence.'

Day after day in a heated, stuffy courtroom in the city's Guildhall they had to keep track of who did what, when, where and with whom. It was intended to clarify matters when Owen Griffiths QC, for the prosecution, told them that if only one man was accused on a particular charge they could draw the inference that others of the seven had been involved because they were 'operating as a team or a gang. Call it what you will.' Clarification or not, they faced a challenge in what was to become Cambridge's longest ever criminal trial. It lasted more than six weeks and was reported in the press as The Cambridge Conspiracy Trial.

It was claimed that over sixteen months the gang went on 'an orgy of crime', raiding shops, business and commercial premises, sub-post offices, a dentist's surgery and a cinema, mostly in Cambridge but with a few sorties to Ely, Wisbech and King's Lynn. They were all successful. On each occasion they had come away with something of value – goods or the contents

Entrance to the court, Cambridge Guildhall. The author

of a safe. Safe breaking was a speciality of the gang. They were ripped open at the back or bottom using tools found at the scene. Occasionally, explosives were used. If a safe could not be opened on the premises it was hauled away to be emptied at a more convenient time and place.

The preliminary arrangements were made by 'the brains', the man in the background responsible for information gathering and organisation, then came 'the doers', the men who carried out the jobs, and finally there was 'the salesman' who disposed of the proceeds.

Only seven men, but with a great deal of criminal talent which they had pooled to become a slick, confident outfit. Only seven, because the fewer the people concerned the greater the share for each man and the greater the security.

But when it came to security, or its breakdown, it would take only one.

The brains, the key figure, was a thirty-one-year-old self-employed builder, Edward John 'Ned' Anstee, living in Nuns Way in Cambridge with his wife, Linda, and their three children. The background man, usually taking little or no part in the burglaries themselves, he controlled the two lock-up garages used by the gang. One in Gwydir Street was where the stolen goods were stored. One in Vinery Road was where the safes not blown on the premises were broken open. The rest of the gang, out of awe, called Anstee 'The Man'.

The doers were Melvyn John Prime, Stanley Luke Whitehead, Joseph Samuel Wilks, Graham Charles Flack and John Peter Ronayne. All had addresses on the outskirts of the city. Ronayne, Wilks and Whitehead lived in the same area as Anstee – Kings Hedges.

Thirty-seven-year-old Ronayne, Anstee's second in command, was 'the clever one'. Quick witted, he was glib and a smooth liar. Referred to in court as an educated man, Ronayne was a surveyor. But his education went beyond that. It was he who could tell the good stuff from the rubbish, who knew what was worth stealing, especially useful in a jewel robbery.

The salesman, who also took part in some of the burglaries, was Brian Cox of Stourbridge Grove, Cambridge. And salesmen, as we all know, can talk. In Cox's case he said something which would have been better left unsaid. Griffiths described him as 'inefficient to say the least.'

In January 1976 Cox had got a new girlfriend, Julie Smith. One day a few months later, unwisely, he said to her that he could get her a pair of boots. In court on the opening day of the trial she said: 'He then forgot about them but I reminded him. I had to ask him about twenty times and he only agreed after I had nagged him all day.'

Cox got the key to the garage in Gwydir Street, the so-called 'Aladdin's cave', from Flack and took her there. It was full of stolen goods under plastic bags and sheeting.

She continued: 'I saw a bag with boots in it but I didn't see anything I liked. I also saw a cardboard box with lots of things

Gwydir Street as it was. Cambridgeshire Collection

Gwydir Street in 2007. The author

in it. He just told me to take what I wanted, and I did. I took almost everything in it and put it into a plastic bag.'

Generously, she later gave some of the contents of her plastic bag to her friend, Kathleen, who in turn gave some to her friend, Lesley. And then someone told the police.

The property that Julie Smith had seen in the garage or had taken away with her could hardly have been more incriminating. She had taken away expensive jewellery. That was from the gang's robbery of Parker's in King's Lynn when almost the entire stock of the jewellers had been stolen. She had taken away Christmas cards, wrapping paper and chocolate from the robbery of Cambridge's Norfolk Street sub-post office when the main objective had been the contents of the safe. The boots, which she had been taken to the garage to see and had not liked, were from the burglary of the Fenland Shoe and Fashion Centre in Wisbech.

The first of the many charges related to those three crimes. All seven men were charged with burgling the post office, stealing property worth £3,610, and receiving property stolen there. Cox and Ronayne were charged with stealing and receiving property worth £5,000 from the King's Lynn jewellers. Wilks, Cox, Anstee and Flack were charged with burgling the Wisbech store, stealing goods worth £4,000 and receiving them. Cox and Flack were charged with the disposal of goods from Wisbech and Wilks with possessing a pair of stolen boots.

Similar charges followed relating to other burglaries, implicating all seven men. Whitehead, said to be unemployed, seemed to be involved in more than his share. He was said to have confessed in custody to forty-three robberies including 'doing seven peters', or safes, but he later denied that. Still, it was claimed in court that he had burgled the Regent Street sub-post office, Curtis' butchers, Texas Homecare Centre and Piggott's printers, all in Cambridge, and the Rex Cinema and Co-op store in Ely. He was also charged with the receiving and disposal of stolen property. Ronayne was said to have burgled the National Tyre Company, stealing keys, and the Drill Hall in Cambridge's East Road, stealing £850.

Flack quickly broke ranks. By the third day of the trial he had changed his plea to guilty on charges of helping in the disposal of goods stolen in the Wisbech and Norfolk Street robberies and he was sentenced to two years. But he had not made his last appearance in court.

Six men were left to face twenty-six charges, six men who were said to be always together, always in each other's company, both working and socialising. They were even, according to police, together, in twos or threes, in the early hours of the morning. They denied being close, they hardly knew each other, but Prime admitted that Wilks was 'a pal'.

Anstee and the men he sometimes employed as bricklayers, Prime, Wilks and Cox, had certainly been working together near the post office in Norfolk Street shortly before it had been burgled. Although Wilks called himself a 'general dealer' rather than a brickie. Brickie or not, he was said to have been one of those who had entered through the post office ceiling and prised the back off the safe. Being December, just before the festive season, they had included Christmas cards and wrapping paper in their haul, later taken from the Gwydir Street garage by Cox's girlfriend. Police found more wrapping paper in a shed at Wilks' home, but he denied getting it in the burglary. It was different wrapping paper. He had got it through his father and had been selling it.

Dozens of pairs of boots were lined up in the courtroom for Peter deBoer, owner of the Wisbech shop, to see. Wrapping paper was wrapping paper, hard to tell one sheet from another, but deBoer was able to identify the boots as his from a pair of childrens' fur-lined ones. He said: 'These must be from my shop because nobody else in this country has any. They were made for exporting to Norway and I bought a small cancelled order. I was the only person to have any.' They had been found in the Gwydir Street garage. He also identified as his Wilks' pair of boots.

Ronald Parker, the King's Lynn jeweller, said that his shop had been entered through an adjoining wall and virtually all of his stock had been taken. In court he was able to identify some of the property shown as coming from his shop, the items that Cox had given to his girlfriend and, more damningly for Ronayne, his choice of the good stuff.

One Saturday in March 1976, the Drill Hall in East Road, used by the Post Office Social Club, had been burgled and about £850 taken in notes and change, some of it the bulky and heavy contents of a fruit machine. The next day police found a cash box full of money hidden in a nearby timber yard and four officers lay in wait to see who would come to retrieve it. Detective Constable Harry Rooke said in court that Ronayne had climbed over the gate into the yard at about 6 pm and had gone towards the hidden money. But then things had gone a bit wrong. 'I moved to take up a position by the gate to block any exit. I made a noise.' Ronayne had then stopped going towards the money. He had turned away and the two men had met in the

East Road. The author

middle of the yard. Ronayne had said: 'Hello. What are you doing here?' He said that he had noticed someone in the yard and had thought he should investigate. But none of the officers would have been visible, 'bobbing about'. The answer to Ronayne's question was that he was arresting him.

Later that evening detectives searched Ronayne's flat in Campkin Road. In the bathroom they found £600 in notes wrapped in a towel and hidden at the bottom of a linen basket. He said the money was his life savings. He was a bankrupt and not allowed to have a bank account. The search continued and, underneath a wardrobe in the bedroom, they found a plastic bag full of jewellery and watch straps. He said to police: 'I think I know where this came from. I am being set up.' He said that he had not known it was there. It was a surprise. He was so surprised that he touched some items as they fell onto the bed. He claimed, 'it was a natural reaction to pick it up.' The prosecution view was: 'You did so because your fingerprints were already on them.' 'Rubbish', said Ronayne. His defence asked the members of the jury: 'Does Mr Ronayne look like the sort of chap who would go round pubs trying to flog watch straps?' He would have their reply at a later date, when they returned their verdict.

In the early hours of an April morning police, in response to an activated burglar alarm, raced to the Co-op store in Ely, next door to another of the gang's targets, the Rex Cinema. The alarm had gone off in the store's hardware department as the raiders looked for tools to use to open the safe in the grocery department. £114 had been taken from it by the time the police got there. They had heard sounds of two or three people on the shop roof, but they had got away.

Having their suspects in mind, the police set up road blocks on the routes that gang members may take on their way back into Cambridge and a car was seen to turn off just before one block, in Milton Road. Police chased and stopped the car. In it were Wilks and Prime, their car radio tuned to a police channel. It was 5-30 am. Ely? No. What gave them an idea like that? They had not been to Ely, they said. They had been out drinking together in Cambridge. Afterwards, Prime said, he had driven Wilks to his home in King's Hedges Road but his wife had put his suitcase on the doorstep. Wilks had then asked Prime to drive him to his mother's home in Peverel Road. But when they got there he had changed his mind and Prime was taking him back to his home in King's Hedges Road – which was where the police had stopped the car. Griffiths declared it to be 'a cock and bull story'.

Flack, who had pleaded guilty to two charges and had been given a two year sentence, now returned to the court in a different guise. He reappeared as a witness for the Crown, in some quarters known as 'doing the royals', swearing that Anstee had threatened him with violence. Unwittingly, he had become involved with stolen goods and he had wanted no part of it. In custody he had wanted to tell the police the truth about the contents of the Gwydir Street garage and of his own innocence. And Anstee had known that. While members of the gang had been on remand in Bedford prison Anstee, he claimed, had told him that he could get his legs blown off. Previously he had rejected his offer of bribes.

Flack told the jury: 'He tried to bribe me with money to start with. He offered me money to keep my mouth shut and say nothing about what I'd seen in the garage. He also offered me £1,000 worth of jewellery, but I wouldn't accept it. He said if I didn't keep my mouth shut I'd more than likely get my brains kicked in.' He said that he had believed Anstee and had been frightened of him. There was a suggestion in court that several of the gang had viewed Anstee with what, in the criminal world, was usually termed 'respect'.

Anstee, who did not say a word in court, left the response to his defence, David Calcutt QC. His client had not offered any threats of violence or any bribes. He told Flack: 'You have been untruthful, haven't you?' Flack replied: 'No sir. This is the truth.' Honour – among thieves.

And there was more to come. A 'grass' was introduced to the jury. Charles Eccles Cameron, jailed for nine months at

Cambridge Crown Court in July, found guilty of burglary. He appeared as a witness for the prosecution. He said that he had shared a remand cell with some of the gang members in Bedford prison during May and had heard them talk about their criminal exploits.

The defence suggested that Cameron was lying and had made a statement to the police to get a light sentence. Cameron said that the accused had been free and easy with their stories and seemed very stupid. He had told the police because he had not wanted to get involved with them. 'I wasn't going to get a knock on the door and get stuck with some conspiracy or something.' Named by him as being especially loose-tongued were Prime, Ronayne and Cox.

Cox had already said too much. He had got the gang where it was, and he knew it. As the prosecution case drew to a close he changed his plea to three charges relating to the disposal of stolen goods from not guilty to guilty in a desperate attempt to divert more of the guilt from others onto himself.

He said that he had sold two pairs of boots to Anstee for £10 and had not told him that they were stolen. And he had left a plastic bag of stolen property, jewellery, in Ronayne's flat, putting it under a wardrobe. He had meant to collect it later. He said: 'He never knew the stuff was there, and that's the truth.' Griffiths opinion was: 'Cox is in the cart and he is doing his best to help the co-accused. He is taking the blame.'

His best was hardly likely to be good enough. An agreement had existed between all six of the men and there were similarities in the way in which all the burglaries had been carried out. Add or subtract a man, it was probable that all had been equally involved in everything. A conspiracy in action.

A number of witnesses and forensic experts were called into the witness box to tell their tales of dishonest doings in Cambridge, amongst them the dental nurse who had arrived at her New Square surgery to find the safe with its bottom out, the woman who had sold 17,000 cigarettes stolen from a Silver Street tobacconist to Wilks, abetted by Prime and Whitehead, and the forensic scientist who had found traces of safe ballast in Ronayne's jeans.

On that subject Detective Constable Terry Edwards, who had arrested the Cambridge Rapist just a few months before, had something to say. He had opened the boot of Whitehead's car and had seen what looked like a pile of safe ballast, similar to that from the Texas Homecare safe. Much more than a trace.

He told the court: 'He began to shake visibly at this stage,' something he was to deny to the jury. Whitehead said: 'I was a bit shocked, yes, but I don't think I shook. There was a big pile. A heap. It's a mystery how it got there.'

Anstee, who had kept himself comparatively clean throughout the gang's months of operation, had chosen not to open his mouth in court. His wife, Linda, did not have that choice. Linda Anstee went into the witness box and was asked to go to change her clothes. She was told to put on some of the exhibits in court, a skirt and jacket, taken from her home when the police had made a midnight raid. She had worn them to a wedding. But were they from the burglary of the Fenland Shoe and Fashion Centre? The Crown claimed that they were. If the jury agreed then the cautious Anstee could have at least one charge to answer.

At the end of the trial's fifth week, well into December, the closing speeches began. Together with the judge's summing-up they would take a week. They began with the defence stressing that there had been no evidence of a conspiracy of any kind. The jury was told: 'The so-called Cambridge conspiracy was no more than a hopeful gleam in Inspector Heppleston's eye. Then it all became my eye and Mother Riley.' And of claims that police had gilded some of the evidence: 'If there is a whiff of suspicion use a pair of long tongs to drop the counts out of the jury room window.'

Both sides warned the jury not to get confused by the mass of evidence they had heard over the past five weeks. Confusion would be easy.

When Judge Wild began his summing-up, he told the jury that it was for them to decide whether or not there had been a team of burglars at work. That was the essence of the case they had been listening to. He said: 'This case – if it is about anything – is about burglary. Whether this is or not a team of burglars. That, you may think, is really the essence of the case. The crime of conspiracy is merely the agreement to commit a crime. As short and as sweet as that. It's like a club. You can join it or leave it.'

As his summing-up neared its end he warned the jury to 'come prepared' for what was to be the last day, and their retirement. The next day, Thursday 16 December, he intended to send them out to consider the charges and examine the scores of exhibits before reaching their fifty-plus verdicts, and he was concerned for their welfare. 'I am not sure how you will manage. The facilities in the Guildhall are very bad and because

of the economic climate are likely to remain so for some time.'
It was difficult to bring refreshments into the building, so they
must come prepared.

After a long, stifling morning the jury retired to consider its
many and various verdicts. It was a formidable task. To lighten
the load Judge Wild discharged it from bringing in verdicts on
the charge of conspiracy to handle stolen goods and from giving
verdicts on alternative charges.

It took the jurors eleven hours to reach their decisions. It was
almost midnight when they filed back into court. They had
brought their own flasks and sandwiches and they had done
their duty. They found Anstee, Cox, Ronayne and Whitehead
guilty of conspiring together to commit burglary. Prime and
Wilks, found not guilty of conspiracy, would be found guilty on
other charges, as would all of the accused.

The next morning came the sentencing for the part each man
had played in each of the fifteen crimes under consideration:

Cox and Ronayne – guilty of the disposal of goods stolen from
Norfolk Street post office and Parker's jewellers, King's Lynn.

Cox – guilty of the disposal of goods from the Fenland Shoe
and Fashion Centre, Wisbech.

Wilks – guilty of receiving a pair of boots.

Whitehead – guilty of burgling a number of Cambridge and
Ely premises and stealing money and property from Curtis'
butchers, Texas Homecare, F &P Piggott printers, Hire and Buy
and the Rex Cinema.

Ronayne – guilty of receiving keys from the National Tyre
Company and burgling the Drill Hall.

Prime and Wilks – guilty of burgling Ely Co-op and stealing
from both the grocery and hardware departments. They were
also found guilty of helping in the disposal of stolen cigarettes
but not guilty of taking part in the Norfolk Street robbery.

Anstee, who had masterminded the whole thing, had taken
care not to implicate himself in the burglaries themselves. All
that he could be found guilty of was dishonestly receiving boots,
shoes and clothing from the Wisbech job and property from the
job in Norfolk Street.

Still, his key role as 'The Man' was acknowledged. He was
given the longest sentence of seven years. Cox, Ronayne,
Whitehead and Prime got six years and Wilks four. In all, the
six-man gang was to serve thirty-five years. And it had all come
about because a girl had fancied a new pair of boots.

CHAPTER 11

One for the Pot

1976

Wearing the wellington boot was a dead man.

T
he poet Lord Byron, up at Trinity College in the first years of the nineteeth century, had a zest for life if not for his studies. Swimming in the River Cam, or the Granta as it may be called above Cambridge, was a special pleasure to him, a favourite place being the mill pond of the old Trumpington Mill of Chaucer's *Reeve's Tale* where the shallow flow was deep enough for diving. An idyllic spot on the edge of the village of Grantchester made famous by another later Cambridge student and poet, Rupert Brooke, it had become known as Byron's Pool by the early 1850s.

Byron's Pool and anglers enjoying a day's fishing. Cambridgeshire Collection

On Tuesday 6 January 1976, a cold but sunny New Year morning, an off-duty Essex police constable, twenty-nine-year-old Neil Everard, went there to fish. He had been there the day before and had enjoyed his fishing so much that he had returned for a second day. He had planned to be there early, by 8 am, but he had stayed up late the night before to watch television – the US cop programme *Columbo* had been on – and he had slept in. It had been almost eleven when he had got to the pool.

He saw a dark green car in the parking area, and noticed the anti-blood sports stickers on a window. As he went towards his fishing spot he saw a rod set up on its stand, its line in the water, and beside it an open bait box and a thermos flask. Close by, lying in the mud, was a cine camera. But there was no sign of the angler. Perhaps he was stretching his legs, having a walk. Time went by and he did not return. Perhaps he was not well. Everard retraced his steps along the path and it was then that he noticed signs of something heavy having been dragged from it into the thick undergrowth. The copper in him took over and, looking more closely, he found a pool of blood and what looked like scraps of brain. And then, amongst the leaves and ivy at the base of a tree, he saw a wellington boot.

Wearing the wellington boot was a dead man. He had been shot at close range. Half of his head had been blasted away.

Detective Chief Superintendent Charles Naan, the head of the Cambridgeshire CID, immediately launched a murder investigation. The world-famous beauty spot, just off the Grantchester to Trumpington road, was sealed off and so many police vehicles arrived at the scene that traffic on the road was held up. A communications caravan was towed into the picnic area to join the panda cars and the police dog and diver units.

Professor Austin Gresham, the Cambridge based Home Office pathologist, was called in and he put the time of death at between eight and nine that morning. Later, it would be extended to ten, the time when witnesses said that they had heard up to five shots. The murder had taken place less than an hour before Everard's arrival. Had he not stayed up to watch *Columbo* would he have arrived in time to avert what had taken place or might he have been a victim? They were thoughts that he found sobering. Witnesses had also seen a second car parked alongside the green one earlier that morning. The description of that car gave Everard more than supposition to consider.

Uniformed and plain-clothes officers combed the scene, helped by dog handlers and soldiers from the Royal Engineers

39 Field Regiment based at Waterbeach. They worked their way through the woods and thick undergrowth with metal detectors, looking for the weapon, a shotgun, and cartridges, while frogmen searched the pool. The weapon was not found.

From examination of the body it was determined that the victim had been shot in the back and in the leg, perhaps as he had been running away from his attacker. One shot had been at closer range than the other. And then a third shot, the fatal one, had been fired into his head at such close range that it may have been only inches.

At first, police were unable to identify the victim. There were no personal items on the body. He was wearing a wedding ring but the engraving on it had become too worn to read. His car and the items by the pool eventually provided the information they needed.

Although the car, at first, had caused alarm in its own right. It had Belfast number plates, 6369 WZ, at a time when there had been sectarian killings in Northern Ireland. But the alarm had not lasted long when it became known that the car had changed hands several times before being registered in Cambridgeshire. It was as blameless as the man who owned it. The man was, had been, William John Charles Sweet, a fifty-six year old porter at Girton College. He lived in Byron Square, Trumpington, on the outskirts of Cambridge, with his wife, Stella. They had two grown-up daughters.

For many years Sweet had been a Cambridge greengrocer, first with a shop in Newmarket Road and then with a mobile shop which toured the south of the city. Heart problems had forced him to give that up about a year before his murder and, after a spell in charge of the greengrocery section of a Budgen's supermarket, he had taken the job at Girton.

He was a keen and expert angler, well known in the sport, and for many years he had been a member of the Cambridgeshire team. Despite his poor health, he had remained a competitive angler for the Histon and District Angling Club and the Newton Angling Club, where a trolley had been specially built to carry his fishing gear to enable him to reach his peg more easily. Sweet was also a strong opponent of blood sports and a paid-up member of the League Against Cruel Sports, and police began to think that that may have caused his death. As Naan said: 'It may well be that Mr Sweet heard shots and went to remonstrate with someone either hunting or rough shooting. It is quite possible that a row ensued about blood

sports and that the gunman lost his temper and fired at Mr
Sweet. It was a brutal killing of a man who appears to have been
out only to enjoy a day's fishing.'

But that was not the only theory in the first hours after the
murder. Naan went on: 'The only other immediate possibility is
that the victim was attacked by a maniac roaming the woods
with a loaded shotgun. Because he was out for a day's fishing
Mr Sweet was carrying no cash or valuables other than his
wedding ring, which was still on his finger. Therefore it would
appear that robbery was not a motive.'

The Cambridgeshire force, especially its CID under Naan,
was thorough and efficient. It had proved its worth in the hunt
for the Cambridge Rapist, arrested and charged in June 1975,
and the same incident room was used in the collation of
information about the murder of Sweet. Part of the routine
policing of Naan and his colleagues was to know their patch and
the people in it who had brought themselves to their attention.
They knew their 'likely suspects'. Witnesses had come forward
who had seen a second car parked at the pool on the morning
of the murder. That same car had been seen by PC Everard the
day before. And he had seen its driver. The descriptions of both

The new Cambridgeshire Constabulary headquarters, Parkside.
Cambridgeshire Collection

car and man had been all that Naan had needed.

That evening police called on a young cavity insulator living in Histon Road who had been given a twelve month suspended sentence by Wisbech Crown Court on 4 July 1975 for possessing a firearm and ammunition after committing a crime. Detectives from divisional headquarters raided the home he shared with his wife and two children. After some time inside they left taking with them a dark-haired and bearded twenty-four-year-old – Peter David Littlechild. He was driven straight to Parkside police station for further questioning. His car followed, as also did the washing from the clothes line in his garden, for forensic examination. The murderer must have been bloodstained but, on analysis of the washing, no signs of blood were found.

Interviewed by detectives Naan and Hookham, Littlechild at first said that he had been off work on the day of the murder and had stayed at home. And then, in a second statement, he admitted that he had been at Byron's Pool on both days, the Monday when Everard said that he had seen him and the Tuesday when the murder had taken place. He said that on the Tuesday morning he had been in his car eating sandwiches between 9-15 and 10-15. 'I heard some bangs. I thought they were from the rifle range on Barton Road. I was sure of it.' He said that he had lied in his first statement because he had been frightened and he stressed several times that he would never kill anyone.

But when Naan asked: 'Why did it happen?' it proved too much for him. He broke. He asked if he could phone his wife and then he said: 'I can tell you where the gun is. It is in the river by Stretham Bridge. It's all at Stretham.'

Naan asked: 'What do you mean – it's all there?'

Littlechild replied: 'His watch came off when I was dragging him. He was coming at me and I fired at him.'

Late in the evening, about 10 pm, Mrs Littlechild visited her husband and he admitted to her that he had killed Mr Sweet. A second confession.

'Why?' she asked

'Who knows why?' he answered. 'That's one question I can't answer.'

Mrs Littlechild had known that he had an airgun but she had not known that he owned a shotgun. He said he had had it for a long time.

'It was an accident,' he said. 'If only he had left me alone. I did not mean to kill him.'

When his solicitor arrived Littlechild made a third statement. He gave a full account of what had happened, and Naan had been on the right track with his first theory that Sweet had been angered by Littlechild shooting at birds. Later, it was proved that Littlechild was perfectly sane, disproving Naan's second possibility that there may have been a maniac loose in the woods.

In his account with his solicitor present Littlechild said: 'I had the gun in the boot of my car. I took it out and was just shooting at small birds and tree stumps. I was sort of minding my own business. I was facing the river. Next thing I knew this fellow was ranting and raving and running at me. I didn't even know what he was saying. It went bang. I pulled him into the woods and things kept falling out of his pocket. I just could not believe I had done it. Then I got panicky. His watch came off, his wallet came out of his pocket, and his car keys. I dropped my gun.'

After hiding Sweet's body, Littlechild had picked up the scattered possessions and his gun and run to his car. He had driven frantically away to dispose of them. 'I was very scared. I was going down the A10 and I came to Stretham Bridge and I just threw everything away.'

Back in Cambridge, he had left his car in the Lion Yard multi-storey car park and had thrown his blood-soaked shoes in a litter bin by the Guildhall. He had then had a cup of tea at a cafe in Bradwell's Court. After walking about for a while he had gone to the cinema. The film that he had seen was *Jaws*. 'I sat there crying for most of it. Now I am relieved it's all over. I didn't mean to kill him.' The film and the crying over, he had gone home to his wife and children at 5-30 pm.

Detained in custody overnight, Littlechild went to Stretham with the police the next morning and showed them the spot where he had thrown the shotgun into the River Ouse. Stretham is a lonely village in the flatness of the Cambridgeshire fens, on the road between Cambridge and Ely, and is the site of the last surviving steam engine used in the draining of the fens. Surely, in the cold of that January, it was a bleak spot for such a gruesome police activity.

Divers found live cartridges and one spent one, and the stock and barrel of a sawn-off shotgun.

When Littlechild came before Mr Justice Stocker in early May, four months after the murder, that shotgun, its loading and reloading, would be of the utmost significance to both the prosecution and the defence.

Littlechild pleaded not guilty to murder. He chose not to

speak on his own behalf and remained silent in the dock. He
had, after all, confessed three times that he had shot Mr Sweet
– to his wife, to his brother, Dennis, when he had visited him,
and to the police. The prosecution was to call fifteen witnesses,
the defence none at all. There was no defence to the shooting,
only to the cause.

Through his counsel, John Marriage QC, Littlechild said
that although he had fired three shots, one of which had been
fatal, they had been fired accidentally.

Marriage said: 'On 6 January the defendant drove to Byron's
Pool, Cambridge, and between 9 and 10 am fired a shotgun in
the woods there with the result that the deceased was hit by
pellets and in fact died.'

He claimed that Littlechild had not been taking enough care
as he fired at birds and had accidentally hit Mr Sweet twice as
he had suddenly run at him, incensed that the wildlife was being
killed. Accidentally again, a third shot had hit him, proving fatal.

He asked the jury to consider that, for some reason, Mr
Sweet had stopped fishing, leaving his gear, and had gone into
the nearby woods where, through Littlechild's complete
negligence, he was accidentally shot.

'It is not very difficult to envisage the circumstances of the
defendant shooting twice without taking care.' Then, he went
on, Littlechild, not knowing that he had accidentally hit Mr
Sweet with shotgun pellets, reloaded and went off 'in a world of
his own'. A naturally very irate Mr Sweet may then have run up
behind Littlechild. Marriage asked: 'Is it impossible that the
defendant should swing round and discharge the gun in the face
of Mr Sweet?'

William Howard, prosecuting, responded: 'It may be that the
accused person went to Byron's Pool to shoot pheasants or any
other game that he might see and it may be that his presence
there with a sawn-off shotgun aroused some indignation in Mr
Sweet and perhaps Mr Sweet reproached or even shouted at
him.' Whatever had happened between them came down to the
fact that Littlechild had put his gun close to Sweet's head and
had fired a third shot. Howard said: 'You cannot put a shotgun
within inches of a man's head and then pull the trigger without
intending to kill.'

Geoffrey Bunting, a ballistics expert, and Austin Gresham,
who had carried out the post-mortem on the body, both gave
evidence to clarify what had probably taken place. The first two
shots had been fired at Sweet through a rubber wading boot into

his left leg and across his back, but they had not caused death. In fact, the leg wound was unlikely to have caused Sweet to fall and so it could not be ruled out that he had been standing up, facing his attacker, when he had been shot in the head at a range of less than two yards. It may have been only a few inches as the front left side of his head had been shot away.

Almost the whole of the case for the defence and for the prosecution would rest on that third shot.

The ballistics expert said that the Hungarian-made, double-barrelled shotgun Littlechild had used, was of the ejector type. To be fired three times it would have had to be reloaded. So, in the confrontation with Sweet, either between the shot to the leg and the shot to the back, or between the shot to the back and the one to the head, Littlechild had reloaded.

According to the defence, not one, not two, but three accidental shots had hit William Sweet on that sunny January morning. He had gone to Byron's Pool to fish and to film the birds he loved and, instead, he had met Peter Littlechild and had met his death. Three accidental shots and, at some point, the marksman had reloaded his shotgun. For the prosecution, that was one accidental shot too many.

It was up to the jury to decide if all three shots had been accidental or if any one of them, or indeed all three, had been deliberate. The shot which had killed William Sweet was the determining issue in the case. On that third shot Littlechild would be found innocent or guilty of murder.

The jury found him guilty. Life imprisonment was the sentence.

CHAPTER 12

All that Glitters

1976–77

. . . they were discerning.

In 1976 a gang of raiders was at work in the Cambridge area. In six months, from July 1976 into the New Year of 1977, more than £1 million worth of antiques, paintings, clocks, jewellery and silver – irreplaceable treasures, almost priceless at today's values – was stolen from the country houses, family homes and weekend retreats of the well-to-do throughout the South-East. But Cambridgeshire was the hardest hit region.

There had been a succession of raids in or close to Cambridge. In the city, valuables were taken from six top addresses – in Babraham Road, Barrow Road, Bentley Road, Sedley Taylor Road, Madingley Road and The Westerings, off Newmarket Road. Others, the more lucrative, had been in the out-of-town areas round about. Four more took place in the first five days of 1977.

Rural Cambridgeshire with its many country estates and large number of wealthy, often isolated, properties, could have been specially manufactured for the gang to target. It was ideal.

An added attraction for the thieves, who were thought not to be local, was that they could move in and out of the Cambridge area relatively easily using good, fast roads leading directly to London, the Midlands, or the east coast ports of Felixstowe and Harwich. And all the roads were interlinked, helping the gang's getaway after a raid and the storage or disposal of stolen items.

Many of the raids in Cambridgeshire were on houses close to the A14, or with access to and from roads such as the A603 and A604. Between them they opened up the whole of the area. Police were to find the raiders extremely elusive for that reason. But there were other reasons.

The most significant raids close to Cambridge in the second half of 1976 were at Melbourn Bury, after midnight on Tuesday 10 August, at West Wratting Park in the early hours of Friday 22 October and at Wimpole Hall during the night of Thursday 18

November. Melbourn Bury, the home of Sir Stanley Fordham, a former British ambassador and High Sheriff of Cambridgeshire, was entered between one and three in the morning. A window was forced in the billiard room and the gang then went into the dining and living rooms where items of silver were kept.

But they were discerning. Sir Stanley said: 'They took only the sterling silver and left a considerable amount of foreign silver untouched. They took spoons, forks, salvers, a particularly valuable snuffbox, candlesticks, an inkstand and one or two other pieces. They knew what was good, so to speak, and what was bad.' And it might have been worse. Perhaps they would have gone on to take the foreign silver as well but they had fled, suddenly alarmed, leaving items lying about, perhaps disturbed when Sir Stanley had got out of bed to go to the bathroom.

They must have realised the quantity of valuable items they had left behind because they returned in late November. But something, again, seemed to have alarmed them. On that occasion they did not go into the house. Sir Stanley knew nothing of it. He just found that his phone was out of action, which he reported. The engineers who came to repair it found that the wires had been cut and the police were called. Cambridge detectives had then found that an attempt had been made to cut through the glass of a door, near to where a catch could be lifted to open it. They had obviously stopped for some unknown but fortunate reason just as they had been about to enter Melbourn Bury for the second time.

Widowed Lady Ursula D'Abo, a former Paul Getty hostess, was at her luxury home, West Wratting Park, seven miles from Newmarket, when the gang of robbers struck at about midnight and began to collect together the silver and antiques that they wanted to take.

As they worked, the burglar alarm was activated silently, alerting the police. Four minutes later the audible alarm sounded in the house and the gang made a speedy escape, taking with them the things closest to hand, an antique clock and two pieces of Meissen porcelain. They were gone, back along whatever road they had come by, by the time the police were with Lady Ursula.

Just over three weeks later came the gang's potentially biggest raid of all in the Cambridge area – on Wimpole Hall, Arrington. It was a typical mid-November night. A dripping fog blanketed the 100-room Georgian mansion in its gardens set out by

Wimpole Hall in its isolated, rural setting. Cambridgeshire Collection

Capability Brown and Humphrey Repton. Beyond the gardens were 600 acres of parkland, and beyond the parkland there was an estate of 2,400 acres. Splendour in splendid isolation.

From the 1750s to the 1890s Wimpole Hall had been in the ownership of the Lords Hardwicke. It had then passed into the possession of Lord Clifden who, just before World War Two, had sold it to Captain George Bambridge. A soldier and diplomat, Bambridge was married to Elsie, the only surviving child of Rudyard Kipling. She had continued to live at Wimpole with her companion and her retinue of servants after his death. When she, in her turn, had died, in May 1975, she left the mansion and all its contents, its gardens, park and estate, to the National Trust.

The National Trust accepted the gift in November 1976. It was a major addition to National Trust properties and it was packed with treasures. So pleased was the National Trust that it went overboard with publicity detailing the £2 million worth of art works, porcelain, silver and antiques that it held. Perhaps not a wise thing to do with a gang of thieves known to be on the prowl in the area.

Less than two weeks after the National Trust had trumpeted its acceptance, Wimpole Hall was raided. It had been raided twice before during Mrs Bambridge's ownership. In 1949 a collection of Rudyard Kipling's snuffboxes had been taken and, in December 1967, part of a porcelain collection had been stolen.

The mansion, in the valley of the River Cam, had entertained numerous visitors over the years. Queen Anne had stayed there, and Queen Victoria, and during World War II Eleanor Roosevelt had visited along with a changing population of American servicemen to a one thousand bed emergency hospital in its park. Its visitors on that foggy November night were uninvited.

Under cover of fog and darkness, sight and sound shrouding,

Wimpole Hall. Cambridgeshire Collection

the thieves entered the house by forcing the massive wooden front doors and breaking a pane of glass in an inner door. The break-in was discovered by the butler, William Smith, at 7-43 the next morning. He, of course, alerted the police. They arrived quickly and in force, but far too late. The downstairs rooms had been devastated.

It was the task of a distraught Mrs Kathleen Parker, the former secretary and companion to Elsie Bambridge and still living at Wimpole, to pass on the bad news to the National Trust.

Interviewed later, she said: 'My dog was barking last night but I thought she was barking at an aircraft noise or something like that. The alarm did not go off so I had no cause to think about it. It is awful. I am only glad that it didn't happen while Mrs Bambridge was alive.'

A conservative figure of £100,000 was put on the gang's haul. Some Sir Joshua Reynolds paintings, the collection of Dresden, Worcester and Derby porcelain, Staffordshire pottery, antique clocks and the silver cutlery with the stag's head crest were definitely gone. But what else? The mansion was extensive. So many rooms needed to be looked into. It was impossible at first to have a true idea of what had been taken and it would need a team of experts to work out what had gone and at what value.

Detective Chief Superintendent Charles Naan, the head of Cambridgeshire CID, said the next day: 'It is still too early for us to be able to say with any accuracy precisely what has gone. The place is so vast it will take us quite some time. We are working on a very general estimate of £100,000 but, of course, this could vary up or down depending on what we are told by the experts.' He added: 'This is no one-off job. This was the work of people who knew what they were about and we can say without much doubt that it was not a local gang. It has all the hallmarks of the London outfit who have been doing houses all over the place – Cambridgeshire, Norfolk, Hertfordshire and so on.'

But, as the investigation got fully under way and the experts began to do their job, something unforeseen became apparent. At Wimpole, the gang had missed out on its opportunity of a lifetime because, as Kathleen Parker had said, the alarm did not go off.

Throughout the months during which the antique and silver raids had been taking place the police had faced a problem – the insistence of the insurance companies on early alarms to warn off raiders. Audible alarms in most properties, such as at West Wratting Park, were set to sound four minutes after the inaudible one alerting the police. The idea of the insurance companies was that major losses would be prevented, limiting what the thieves would have the opportunity to take and the amount they would have to pay out. All very well for them. But it also limited the chances of the police catching them. With many of the wealthier houses that were robbed in rural locations, near to that important getaway route but not to the nearest police station, the four minutes had run out while they were still racing to the scene. The thieves worked fast, selecting the most valuable and handiest items first, within that four minutes, and then they were gone.

They had done that at Wimpole Hall without knowing that the burglar alarm was faulty. No one had known that. It had not alerted the police and, when the four minutes were up and the gang was speeding away, it had not sounded in the house and alerted the staff. All had slept soundly – except Mrs Parker's dog. The faulty alarm denied the police any chance they might have had of intercepting the gang as they left, perhaps along the A603, the Cambridge to Bedford road that Wimpole was on. They would not have reached the house in time to prevent the gang's leaving, but they may have been able to set up road blocks. There were a lot of maybes, or to recall Kipling's most famous and best-loved poem, a lot of 'ifs'.

When the loss assessors had done their job the insurers could afford to smile, if not the police. Instead of the estimated £100,000 loss what had been taken was valued at only £18,350. The most valuable items taken were two Joshua Reynolds paintings worth £1,500 – in 1976.

But what had gone wrong at Wimpole? The only occupants of the house were a few elderly staff, old retainers, left to caretake during the mansion's closure pending its handover to the National Trust. The burglar alarm had not been working properly for a while, but there had been no one there to tell them that. One part of the system had been showing a warning light for a long time but it had been misread by the staff as an indicator that all was working well.

Police made enquiries around Wimpole, going house-to-house, although there were not many of those about. The fog had made even the end of the garden out of sight. No one had seen or heard anything. And all that was learned from an examination of the grounds was that the gang had used a van. Hardly unexpected. Another dead end.

And yet, so much was, after a year of robberies, known about the gang. As 1976 reached its end the police should have been closing in, getting ready to make arrests. They knew a great deal, but just not enough. They lacked that essential – proof.

First of all, the police knew that 'the gang' could in fact be as many as three different gangs. They knew that one gang was operating from just north of Kettering and was disposing of its loot through one-day antiques fairs in the Birmingham area and throughout the midlands. Items were stored in barns or warehouses for gradual introduction to the market or, if of special worth or easily recognisable, they were driven straight to the east coast ports. But no items had been recovered. Naan's advice to those who had lost their family treasures was that they should visit the one-day fairs themselves on the lookout for items they knew were theirs. If they spotted any they were to go immediately to the nearest police station. Good advice, but it bore no fruit. And neither did police surveillance.

The other two gangs were based in North Hertfordshire and Stepney, in east London. Police believed that they were the most active. But they were very different in the way they worked. One operated discreetly and effectively, mainly during the day. The other gang relied on surprise and speed, storming in 'like a panzer regiment' and then out again.

But, however they operated, the gangs knew what they were about. Their pre-raid research and information gathering was immaculate, correct in every detail. Of family homes, they knew when the occupants left and when they were likely to return. And they knew what was worth stealing inside the house. In some cases, there had been a caller to the house just before the robbery. Had the gasman really been the gasman? Police recommended that all householders should ask for identification before admitting any caller not personally known to them.

To that suggestion Naan added that householders should have a detailed description of the lost items. 'It is extremely difficult for anyone other than the owner to make a positive identification unless hallmarks, manufacturer's numbers or even repair marks, are known and can be checked.'

For the larger properties, the county's statelier homes, admission to the kitchens to check the electricity meter would not usually provide much information on the what and where of the valuables contained in the house. Most owners would not, unlike the National Trust, give the necessary details out in the national press, but many were flattered to have themselves and their homes featured in one or other of the up-market glossy magazines of the day, such as *The Field* or *Country Life*. The gangs, it was certain, read every issue, cover to cover.

Besides knowing about the gangs, the police also knew the identities of some of the gang members. But they needed more than that. More than they had been able to get. They needed evidence to put before a jury and that was proving impossible to come across.

With raids being carried out all over the South East, many individual police forces were involved, but a central point to which all information was sent and collated was being operated by Surrey police at Walton-on-Thames. Regional crime squads had also been brought in and, covering Cambridgeshire and the eastern counties, was Number 5 Regional Crime Squad based at Hatfield. Its officers liaised with the different forces and also with the Metropolitan Police Art Squad. That rather grand sounding squad was just three officers in a tiny room at New Scotland Yard. Its main task was to gather information about the art works, antiques and silver stolen rather than to be an operational police unit. Over the past few months it must have been swamped. No time for putting the feet up.

A spate of raids ended the year. Perhaps it was the festive spirit. The second attempted raid at Melbourn Bury happened four days after the robbery at Wimpole Hall and, two weeks after that, two more country houses on the same road as Wimpole were raided, just over the county boundary into Bedfordshire. Four days later another attempt was made to rob the home of Christopher Fordham, a cousin of Sir Stanley, at Odsey, just off the main A505.

The first few days of 1977 were just as busy for the gang. Over the Christmas and New Year period four homes were robbed, including that of one of Europe's leading racehorse owners, Charles St George, in Newmarket. Several more raids followed in February. They seemed endless. Amazing that so much of value was there for the taking in and around Cambridge.

In April thieves struck twice in a week in Barton Road, Cambridge, on the second occasion raiding the home of the explorer and scientist Sir Vivian Fuchs. Both he and Lady Fuchs were at home but the robbery was not discovered until the next morning. A table, two silver vases and a ceremonial sword were taken.

Two or three weeks later, in early May, another National Trust property was raided – Anglesey Abbey, formerly the home of Lord and Lady Fairhaven, between Cambridge and Newmarket. At about 3 am on Monday 9 May raiders were

Anglesey Abbey. Cambridgeshire Collection

drilling their way into the finest part of the house, the Oak Room, when they triggered an alarm linked to the police station. Predictably, only four minutes later, the lights came on automatically throughout the house and the alarm was raised. The raiders left, pausing only to grab sixteen antique pistols.

The National Trust administrator and custodian of the property, Captain Reg Cole, said: 'Nothing has gone which will rock the antiques world.' They were valued at £3,500. He was pleased, the National Trust was pleased as, no doubt, were the insurance company. But were the police?

As on so many occasions the police had missed the gang because the early alarm had given it a head start. At Anglesey it had been prevented from getting away with a large haul of priceless antiques. Captain Cole could be pleased that 'nothing had gone'. But, for the police, 'nothing' had a different meaning.

Would they ever be given the few minutes more that they needed to catch the gang? The cells were ready and waiting.

The A603, Cambridge Road at Wimpole. The author

CHAPTER 13

The Luck of the Draw

1970s

. . . a more dangerous place to be than Glasgow

Mid and East Anglia, far away from the big urban areas with their big football clubs, the giants of the English soccer world, could have been expected to be isolated from the rampaging violence of fans, at the grounds and anywhere that they showed up with their scarves and their chants and their pieces of brick, that was marring the sport in the 1970s. But not so. Soccer hooliganism was a national problem affecting society in general. It spread over heath, fen and furrow to reach the quietest corners of Cambridgeshire.

In August 1970, Cambridge United were promoted into the Football League. It was an achievement after years of struggle.

Cambridge United's Abbey Stadium. The author

The club had earned it, and the loyal fans who had stuck with them through thick and mostly thin. It should have delighted them that in an area with no league football nearer than Norwich or Ipswich they would have more exciting games to watch. But, from the first league match, a section of the club's supporters began as it meant to go on – with a hail of any missiles that came to hand. For the aggressive minority the entertainment was not on the pitch.

Week after week, month after month, season after season, throughout the 1970s, war broke out in Cambridge whenever United were playing at home. Public houses were targeted and coaches were stoned, windows were smashed, houses, shops and cars were damaged, anything throwable was thrown and boots and fists were used.

Newmarket Road, the route that many supporters used on their way to and from the Abbey Stadium, bore the brunt, its shopkeepers and residents pleading time and again with the police to make more arrests and to the courts to hand out stiffer punishment.

In August 1976, after six years of league football and hooliganism, a Newmarket Road shopkeeper said: 'I've seen policemen arguing with these hooligans in the street. Why don't they arrest them and let them do their arguing either in the police station or in the court? They give them a ticking off and as soon as they're gone the bricks start flying through the air.'

A man with a home in Newmarket Road who had been threatened twice by fans said: 'We are here and we have to live with the bricks, the fights, the filthy language and the threats. It seems to me that the police are more willing to argue than arrest and, when they do, the courts let them off lightly. Joe Public is left like the piggy in the middle. On the one hand the police can't protect us and on the other the courts don't back them up when they do.'

'What does a suburban housewife or a business man on the bench know about these louts? The nearest they get to them is when they come before them in the court in their best gear, with their hair combed, a good lawyer and a fistful of social workers' reports. What chance do we stand? The court ends up more sorry for them than for us.'

In that same month, August 1976, road works in Newmarket Road provided ammunition for a stone throwing street battle involving twenty fans on each side and a minibus somewhere in the middle while the police were dealing with another stone throwing incident nearer to the football ground. A senior police officer said: 'A van with half a dozen policemen went down there. Being a long stretch of road we can't have men everywhere at once. The police are always out in force to control soccer hooliganism.'

There was a repeat of the violence after a mid-week evening match ten days later when Cambridge beat Oxford 2-0 in one of their best performances. The trouble was all caused by teenaged United fans.

Chief Inspector Jack Cole, Deputy Cambridge City Police Commander, stunned by what he experienced at the first match he had attended, said: 'We expected them to come along Newmarket Road. Instead, they headed for Ditton Walk and smashed on the bus.' A parked Oxford coach had had all its windows broken. 'The trouble is caused by a small group of United supporters, all about sixteen, seventeen and eighteen, who are hell-bent on violence. We have got to take positive action to stop them. We are left with no alternative. We have got to do this for the benefit of the real supporters and ordinary people who go to see a game of football. They don't want a brick

Newmarket Road, close to the Abbey Stadium. The author

wrapped round their ear.' On that occasion three youths were arrested.

Each year from 1970 police spokesmen, some high-ranking, had said much the same as Cole. It was promised that the problem would be dealt with, it would get special attention, action against the hooligans would be stepped up. The words were said, but nothing positive had ever been done. Once again, after Cole's statement, the people of Newmarket Road waited to see if action would be taken and, if so, if it would be backed up by the courts.

There was as much violence inside the Abbey Stadium as in the streets around it. The terraces, especially behind the goal at the Newmarket Road end, the 'kop', heaved. At a match against Colchester on 20 November an eight year old Cambridge boy had to be taken to Addenbrooke's Hospital after being hit on the head by a meat hook thrown at the Colchester goal by the ABBEY BOOT BOYS. (That soubriquet, and others, appeared on walls all over Cambridge.) That day, five meat hooks, steel combs, screws, nails, keys and stones were recovered by police officers.

But the trouble did not end there. It continued outside the ground after the match. Superintendent Harry Gelsthorpe said: 'After the match a crowd of about fifty Cambridge supporters in an obviously ugly mood marched down Newmarket Road.' Violence had broken out once again – and with it the windows – as a mob surged back and forth across the road. 'When officers went in to break it up the crowd seemed to be running amock and an officer was seriously hurt.'

Twenty-five-year-old Police Constable Tony Mason had followed the eight year old lad with the meat hook in his head to Addenbrooke's with head injuries and a serious groin injury from being kneed. When thought to be recovering after a spell in hospital he suffered a collapse and had to be rushed back.

A sixteen year old was arrested for the attack on Mason. Six others were also arrested.

Was it the police or was it the magistrates letting the hooligans get away with the mayhem they were causing? Cambridge United club secretary, Colin Benson, had no doubts. It was the magistrates. 'Some of the sentences they hand out are quite ludicrous. We and the police do all we can but we are just not getting the backing by magistrates that is needed to stamp out violence.'

The Cambridgeshire Chief Constable, Mr Frederick

Drayton Porter, speaking, also in November 1976, on the increase in crimes of violence in general in the city and the fact that being arrested by the police was no longer the deterrent it once had been, said: 'There is little the police service can do except to ask for the full support of the courts in dealing with offenders charged with this type of crime.'

Two months later, on Thursday 7 January 1977, five teenagers, including a fifteen year old girl, appeared before magistrates in Cambridge accused of rampage in Newmarket Road. They had vandalised cars and a telephone box and had broken windows. One couple had returned home to find their front window smashed and a flashing road lamp lying on their lounge carpet. The young louts were fined £20 each and bound over to keep the peace, and their parents were fined and bound over to control their children.

United fans, at that time, should have been focussing on the football at the Abbey Stadium instead of looking for 'sport' of their own. In the New Year of 1977 United were going well under manager Ron Atkinson. At the end of January they were four points clear at the top of Division Four and bookmakers were making them odds-on to finish top of their division and gain promotion to Division Three. Trouble makers apart, they had a stalwart following of local supporters and 3,874 turned out on Saturday 29 January to stand on the freezing terraces of the Abbey and watch them play promotion rivals Darlington.

It was a day when eleven terrorist bomb blasts ripped through London's West End as an IRA protest marked the fifth anniversary of Bloody Sunday. Football hooligans apart, the once-peaceful university town of Cambridge was becoming an increasingly violent place to be, but at least it had not come to that. A student chopped with an axe as he walked across Midsummer Common. A soldier kicked unconscious in Newmarket Road. A stream of victims of motiveless attacks ferried to A and E at Addenbrooke's to be patched up and stitched. That was Cambridge. Just a month before, the choristers of King's had sung of a baby, away in a manger, of hope for the world, of peace, while violence stalked the streets of the city making it a more dangerous place to be than Glasgow.

The day of the match against Darlington was bitterly cold. There was heavy snow in some areas and it was on its way to Cambridgeshire. There had been frost, ice on the roads, and a few wintry showers. It was a day for those who could to stay warm at home. But the Cambridge United fans, used to icy blasts off the fens, had enjoyed a good match and a 4-0 win. It had been worth the foot-stamping time in the cold, muffled to the ears. And, for once, there had been more exultation than aggro on the terraces and in the streets. It was heady stuff in January 1977. United were on a winning streak and that match against Darlington – well, they'd shown 'em, hadn't they!

As if United were on their way to winning the World Cup, two car-loads of young, male United fans took to the streets in jubilant mood. But, suddenly, that jubilation turned to belligerence when they spotted some Wolverhampton Wanderers fans. A coachload of them. And a mini-bus. They were invaders in their territory and, worse, Wolves were so high above United in football terms that they were out of sight. They were the big time. Perhaps that riled.

In their two cars they followed the mini-bus and grabbed a trailing scarf. They threw an aerosol can at the coach. They stopped for a moment and one of the passengers in one of the cars, sixteen year old Andrew Dunn, an apprentice asphalter living on a local Cambridge estate, Ditton Fields, got out to pick up part of a brick. And then they drove past the Wolves

Maid's Causeway. The author

supporters again.

The coach had been driven the fifty miles from Ipswich where Wolves had played The Tractor Boys in the Fourth Round of the FA Cup and had drawn 2-2. With a by-pass still to be completed and opened they had had to come into the city down Newmarket Road and it had been decided that Cambridge was a good place to stop for a bite to eat and a drink before the long drive back to the Midlands through ice and snow. They had stopped at a pub in Maid's Causeway, where Newmarket Road passed Midsummer Common and came to an end, close to the grounds of Jesus College. The small pub could not accommodate all of the fifty or sixty people in the warmth of its bars so some were on the pavement outside, eating and drinking, enjoying the last hours of a companionable day out. And then the car had driven by.

The words of John Archer QC, for the prosecution at Dunn's trial at Norwich Crown Court on 2 June 1977, tell what happened next:

As the car drove past at more than 40mph there was a group of Wolverhampton supporters walking along the road and outside a public house in Newmarket Road. The defendant levered himself out of the window of the car and, sitting partly out of the window, he threw the brick at the group. The brick struck the victim at the base of the skull behind the left ear and he died.

A chance blow. As pathologist Professor Austin Gresham told the inquest: 'The external injury was a large bruise on the upper left side of the neck. This is a very unusual injury, unique in my experience, and not very well recorded. Otherwise, he was a normal, healthy young man. It must have been caused by a blunt, rough object travelling with considerable kinetic energy because of the intense local damage to the neck muscle and the acute extension of the neck being thrown backwards.'

Gerald Thomas Comerford, a twenty-one-year-old salesman from Dudley, Worcestershire, had been hit and had gone down, one moment downing an after-match drink with his mates, the next a corpse. He would not see the replay at Molyneux.

Dunn was quickly arrested. In his statement to the police he said: 'We went past some old boys and they started throwing things at us and I threw the brick and saw him go down.' There was no evidence that anything had been thrown by the Wolves fans and witnesses said that the United fans had gone out with the intention of 'bricking' the coach. Dunn never denied that he had thown the brick, and he faced the consequences, pleading not guilty to murder but guilty to manslaughter.

He was defended by John Blofeld QC, the brother of cricket commentator Henry, who said: 'Everyone must recognise that football violence is an appalling phenomenon and only too prevalent. And courts have a duty to deal with it severely as it can lead to appalling incidents. Mr Dunn recognises this and nothing I can say can detract from the very seriousness of it. He is appalled at what he has done. He never paused to think that by throwing this brick he might kill someone.'

The judge, Mr Justice Gibson, told Dunn: 'This is a grave offence and you and others like you must know that the court will deal with such conduct and punish severely.'

The taking of a life may be the farthest thing from a soccer hooligan's mind but the threshold between life and death is a narrow one. As Dunn found out, it can take little to cross that threshold. One blow. Bad luck.

He was sentenced to three years detention at a place to be decided by the Home Secretary.

And Cambridge United? At the beginning of May, while Dunn had been waiting to stand trial, they had beaten Doncaster Rovers 3-0 and had ensured promotion to Division Three with three matches in hand.

On Saturday 14 May the biggest crowd of the season at the Abbey Stadium, 7,795, saw Cambridge United receive the Fourth Division champion's cup and proudly show it off to their ecstatic supporters. There was a carnival mood.

Perhaps the club's success, the sobering, needless death of a Wolves supporter and Dunn's forthcoming trial, had brought about a change for the better in behaviour. The club, the police, the peaceable majority of the spectators, and everyone the length of Newmarket Road and in the streets around the stadium, hoped so.

The match was against Swansea. After five minutes Swansea scored, the mood changed as if with the flick of a switch, and the mayhem began. Before the match ended, with United losing 2-3, there had been fights behind both goals, fans thrown over the barriers and barriers knocked down, and two pitch invasions. The match itself had also turned sour with players from both sides sent off.

The next season, the one in Division Three that was

supposed to bring better football to Cambridge, saw mob rule, ABBEY AGGRO, reach new heights. United supporters fought with visiting supporters at every match and, at Peterborough, they even turned on themselves. More than four hundred Cambridge United fans fought each other in a bloody battle that the Peterborough fans watched in shocked silence. After the match the battle continued in the car park until they were bundled onto their coaches and sent on their way back to Cambridge.

Did the club's supporters feel that they should behave like animals? After all, six days before, after repeated disruption to matches, injuries, damage to the stadium and pitch invasions, the Cambridge United directors, in desperation, had decided to fence in the ABBEY BOOT BOYS and the ABBEY LOUTS CLUB. The terraces behind both goals at the Abbey Stadium were to be turned into cages, ten foot high steel and mesh barriers penning them in.

In real 'Roy of the Rovers' style the club would continue to go from height to height. The impossible dream would come true – promotion yet again – promotion to Division Two for the 1978-79 season. The future was as rosy as the glow from the flags being burned on the terraces.

That was soccer in Cambridge in the 1970s. Perhaps it was a miracle that only one man, an innocent bystander, had died. And all for the kick of a ball.

Blofeld had called soccer violence an 'appalling phenomenon' and had said that the courts had a duty to deal with it, but no one seemed ready to make the first moves. The courts could only play their part when the hooligans had been arrested and put before them.

A year and a death since Cole had promised 'positive action' against the offenders the householders and shopkeepers of Newmarket Road were still waiting for the promised 'something will be done.'

ABBEY RULE – OK?

CHAPTER 14

By an Evil Chance

1977

Glenn did not return home last night.

Glenn Thompson of Grays Grove in the village of Little Staughton, to the west of St Neots, was almost sixteen. In a couple of months time he would leave school. He was looking forward to that and to the job he had waiting for him in a local engineering works. For him, it was the ideal job. He loved machinery and tinkering about with motorcycles and bicycles. He had turned that into a profitable hobby. He would pick up, at a bargain price, a bike needing work done to it, restore it to good working order, and then sell it on at a profit. It was a handy little income and he enjoyed doing it.

It was that hobby that took him from home at about six in the evening of Saturday 16 April 1977. He had something to eat and then he set off on his bike telling his parents, Alan and Ann Thompson, that he was going to visit his friend, Moses Smith, at his gypsy encampment just outside the village, alongside the road to Kimbolton. They had been friends for a long time and Glenn often went there. He told his parents that he was going to buy an old moped from Moses and that they were going to work on it together.

Glenn did not return home that night.

Ann Thompson said: 'We knew that once before Glenn had gone off for two or three days without telling us after an argument. He had gone to Bedford to see some friends. We wondered if the same thing had happened this time, though there hadn't been any row. I went looking for him on Sunday morning, but no one had seen him.'

It was not until Sunday evening that the family had any idea that something dreadful may have happened to him. 'My daughter, Karen, came in crying. She said that a body had been found in a ditch near the village.' Karen was fourteen. She had been told the news by another girl. Glenn had a second sister, eleven year old Andrea. The whole family had been alarmed.

They had got in touch with the police at once and then had begun, for all four of them, the horrific journey towards the truth.

At about 8 pm police called to confirm their fears. It was Glenn's body. But Alan Thompson, a stockman who was off work ill, had feared the worst all along. He said: 'I knew he was going to die when his picture fell off the wall the other day.'

Glenn had been battered about the head, his head had been covered by a sack held in place by a shoelace, and his body had been dumped in a deep ditch about two and a half miles from his home and quarter of a mile from the nearest house. It had been found by two horsewomen riding by. They rode regularly close to the village. They were sisters, Julie and Suzie Topham, aged twenty and eighteen, who lived at Rectory Farm in Little Staughton. The day after their discovery they were still too upset and ill to speak publicly about it. It was their mother, Violet Topham, who said: 'It was before lunch, at about 12-45 pm. They saw a bike, and then the boy, who wasn't moving. They asked him if he was all right and he didn't say anything so they stopped a passing motorist who called for help.' They had been very lucky that a motorist had come by. The road between Little Staughton and Pertenhall was very quiet. It was more like a winding country lane with little traffic.

The head of Bedfordshire CID, Detective Chief Superintendent John Grant, was put in charge of the murder investigation leading a squad of twenty detectives. An incident room was set up at Bedfordshire police headquarters and an incident caravan was brought into Little Staughton and placed near the village pub.

The body had been taken to Bedford South Wing Hospital and a post-mortem was carried out by Professor J Malcolm Cameron of the London Hospital in Whitechapel, in east London, later that Sunday evening. It could only confirm what was already known – that Glenn had died of head injuries, several heavy blows from a then-unknown weapon.

Detectives went house-to-house in the village and a questionnaire was distributed throughout the area. But, from the start, the police had known who their prime suspect for the murder was. Moses Smith, Glenn's gypsy friend.

He was not in his encampment. He had disappeared by the time the body had been found early on the Sunday afternoon and police in five counties – Bedfordshire, Cambridgeshire, Northamptonshire, Hertfordshire and Essex – were combing gypsy camps and sites looking for him.

Headline: Police Search for Gypsy. Hunts Post

Like Glenn, Moses was fifteen. He was a heavily-built lad with thick, dark brown and wavy, collar-length hair. He was quiet, pleasant and well mannered, as Glenn was, and he valued their friendship. Mr Thompson said: 'They played together a lot. They had known each other for some years. Glenn always respected him and never called him a gypsy. Several times Moses wrote to us and said what a nice family we were. He always seemed very polite and seemed a nice boy.'

Glenn was popular in the village. He went to the local youth club every Friday, was keen on football, and had no trouble making friends. Moses was not so fortunate.

Moses' family moved about from one roadside camp to the next through Bedfordshire, Cambridgeshire and adjacent counties. But they stayed in one place during the winter months. For a number of years they, along with several other families, had made their winter encampment just outside the village of Little Staughton.

With April, spring, and the prospect of better weather, it was almost time for the Smith family to be on the road again. And Moses had not wanted that. More than anything he had wanted to be like Glenn and like all the other village boys. He did not want to be a gypsy, living in a caravan, always moving on. He wanted a place that was home. He wanted to live in a nice house and to sleep in a clean, warm bed every night, and he wanted to go to school.

He had tried going to the local comprehensive. Glenn had attended Margaret Beaufort School in Riseley. He had been thrilled to be in school, like other boys his age, but he had left in tears after he had been taunted and called such things as 'dirty gypsy'.

He craved village life. He hung about Little Staughton all day and only went back to his camp when darkness fell and Glenn and the other lads went home for the night. Of all the lads in the village Glenn Thompson was his firm friend, his best friend.

When they met that Saturday evening in April Glenn offered Moses £2 for the moped, but Moses wanted £5. They had words about it. A trivial disagreement between friends, such as teenagers have. But, in the course of it Glenn did something that he had never done before. He called Moses 'a gypsy'. It was to cost him his life.

Police swooped on the roadside gypsy camp. Hundreds of uniformed officers, some with dogs, were brought in to augment the murder squad, radiating out from the camp to make an intensive search of the area. Seven adults from the caravans, including women, were taken in for questioning. One man was detained for further cross-examination. Others, to distance themselves from the police activity, moved their caravan to another roadside verge about a mile away. None of them were to leave the vicinity. It was a bad time to be a gypsy as suspicion of complicity fell on all of them. Although not implicated in the murder itself any of them might have arranged the killer's disappearance. With strong family and friend networks it was felt that other gypsies, somewhere, had taken Moses in, had given him refuge.

Questioning and searching was still going on when, five days after the murder, an exhausted Moses staggered into a garden in Essex. The man working in the garden was an off-duty policeman.

Before Mr Justice Willis at St Albans Crown Court on Tuesday 6 September, Moses Smith pleaded guilty to the murder of Glenn Thompson and the tragic events of that April evening were recounted.

They had argued over the price of the moped, he told the court. He had been holding the heavy hammer he used when chopping wood for his family's campfire and he had hit Glenn, several times, shattering his skull. There had been so much blood that he had tied a sack over Glenn's head. He had then dragged the body a quarter of a mile, across a field and over a barbed-wire fence, before hiding it in the secluded ditch. He had hidden Glenn's bike in another ditch nearby.

As Brian Escott-Cox QC, defending Moses, said: 'Everyone who knew Smith said he was a quiet, polite and well behaved boy. He and Glenn Thompson were the best of friends. They fell out over a small boyish argument. The attack was triggered off when Thompson called Smith a gypsy. He is very, very sensitive about being called a gypsy. By an evil chance he was holding the hammer in his hand and he lost all self-control.'

Moses was ordered to be detained at Her Majesty's pleasure.

CHAPTER 15

It Wasn't Like That on the Telly

1977

Regan and Carter would never have done that.

Afficionados of British television cop series must remember *The Sweeney* which ran through the second half of the 1970s. John Thaw as Detective Inspector Jack Regan and Dennis Waterman as Detective Sergeant George Carter starred in scores of episodes featuring fast-moving, hard-hitting escapades based on the activities of the Metropolitan Police's elite crime fighting unit, the Flying Squad. The stars made a brilliant double act and the series was popular, true-to-life viewing.

Formed in 1919, to combat serious post-war crime with a speedy response, the real Flying Squad was, from the start, a hit-em-quick force of top detectives using the fastest vehicles available which, like royalty, they usually did not drive themselves as they made their crime busting swoops. They were driven by specially trained police officers, the Formula One men of the force. Wherever crime was, they were there.

When not 'flying' they were quite often doing the opposite, hiding, watching and waiting, ready to fly. Trained in covert surveillance they would patiently carry out an observation, for days if necessary, even for weeks. Their surveillances were often made in response to 'information received'. Informants, or 'snouts', were the life-blood of the Flying Squad. Every officer had his own snouts, not the pleasantest of men to deal with but an indispensable commodity if the Flying Squad was to keep abreast of professional criminals and their activities and, in particular, of the gangs of armed robbers.

The Flying Squad reputation was built on its effectiveness in dealing with the gangs and its exploits had quickly become the stuff of myth and legend. It was given the nickname The Sweeney, from the cockney rhyming slang for Flying Squad – Sweeney Todd – out of respect and perhaps, in some quarters, fear.

But no matter how many criminals they put in the cells, 'banged to rights', there were always more chancers to take their place. And more.

In the 1970s, in London especially, armed robberies of banks and security vans increased to such an extent that there was a possibility they might get out of hand. The Flying Squad was needed more than ever before and, courtesy of its snouts, it had some stunning successes, racing in to capture gangs red-handed, in mid-raid. Thank God for the Sweeney!

Its unique crime-busting style put the Flying Squad on the front pages of the nation's newspapers and that had led to the dramatisation of its exploits on television. *The Sweeney* made exciting viewing as, week after week, Regan and Carter got their man – or men. It was real. It was what really happened in the Flying Squad.

Or was it? Let's see.

In mid-August 1977, a couple in their forties, Peter and Pat Worbey, took over the Autostop Transport Cafe in the Cambridgeshire settlement of New Wimpole. It was a good place for a transport cafe, close to the A603 and not far from the busy A14. Two and a half weeks later they were feeling settled in and had begun to get to know the regular customers who stopped by for a break and refreshments.

On 5 September, two customers came in who were not any of the regulars they had got to know so far, and they did not seem to be the usual 'truckies'. Their behaviour made them memorable.

At about noon the first man had driven onto the cafe forecourt in a silver Ford Cortina saloon. In his forties, he had been well-dressed in a dark blue blazer and wearing a collar and tie. His dark, slightly greying hair had been well groomed, combed straight back, and he had worn glasses. He had been served by the couple's seventeen-year-old daughter, Tricia, but he had seemed more interested in questioning her than in refreshment.

She later said: 'The first man just asked questions, like how long we had been there and what trade was like. He drank a cup of tea at the counter and left. He didn't sit down and I thought it was all a bit odd.'

Tricia had still been behind the counter when the second man had come in at about two o'clock. He had not even wanted a cup of tea. He had only been desperate to use the phone.

Tricia remembered it well. 'Then the second man came in. He had overalls on and wellington boots. He was agitated and

Cambridge Evening News

NIGHT FINAL

TUESDAY, SEPTEMBER 6, 1977   No 27,340   Price 7p

CAMBS HOLD-UP DRAMA

Gun gang raid foiled

A gang of six men armed with shotguns tried to rob a Security Express van carrying £200,000 in cash in a Cambridgeshire village yesterday.

But they fled when the guards, who escaped unhurt, set off their alarm. No shots were fired.

The drama took place on the forecourt of the Autostop transport café in New Wimpole, where the three security men had pulled in for refreshments.

A bulldozer driver, Mr Andrew Green, who was working on a site opposite the café, heard the van alarm go off.

He told the "News": "I didn't see anything so I thought it was an electrical fault or something. But then I saw a bloke with his hands in the air, and I knew it must be some sort of raid.

"I started to go across the field and the raiders jumped into a brown Ford Cortina and made off.

"When I spoke to the security men who had been in the van they said that at one stage they turned round to find guns pointing at them through the back of the van."

The Autostop Café was taken over two and a half weeks ago by Mr Peter Worbey and his wife, Pat. They saw nothing of the raid, but their daughter, Tricia, aged 17, saw the tail end of the activity.

● Full report—page 3.

Andrew Green — he saw the robbers make off.

A relieved Tricia Worbey after the ordeal. She was warned to stay out of their way.

MASKED GANG STEALS IRISH MAIL

An armed and masked gang stole mail from a car, two Post Office vehicles and a lorry in a raid early today on Sligo railway station in the Irish Republic.

Up to 10 men were involved in the incident but no-one was hurt. The mail stolen by the gang is understood to include cash due to be paid out today in children's allowances.

The gang swooped in an apparently split-second-timed operation as mail was being unloaded from a train.

The gang took all the mail and drove away a police car which was to have escorted a mail lorry to nearby Leitrim.

Irish troops later joined in the search for the gang. Road blocks were operated in three counties.

Power strike break claim

Power station workers accused engineers of strike-breaking today as their 48-hour unofficial stoppage failed to bring early power cuts.

It had been feared strike—launched at 10 last night—might bite into industry.

But as the morning passed without trouble, Electricity Council said was "cautiously optimistic".

A spokesman for East Electricity at their Mill Hill headquarters said: are just holding out at moment.

"It looks as though might get away with dropping the voltage and, maybe, having to disconnect one for three hours."

Water supplies

Workers from four unions called the 48-hour strike from 10 p.m. last night in support of claims for an increase in shift pay from £5 to £10 a week, free transport to and from work, and concessionary fuel.

The Anglian Water Authority today emphasised the need to cut water consumption during a power strike.

At the same time it announced that emergency measures taken by the Anglian Water Company should ensure there is no disruption of supplies during the power strike.

But a lot depends on the reduction in consumption and the company's deputy manager, Mr R. Burgin, said he hoped there would be no reduction in supplies.

TUC declares war on Grunwick

The TUC today declared war on Grunwick — the embattled North London film processing plant.

And before the Congress delegates showed their unanimous support for the strikers on the second day of their Blackpool conference, the union leader at the centre of the year-long dispute gave warning of a "speedy end".

Mr George Ward's firm. Meetings are due to start next week to try to impose a trade blockade of Grunwick and bring the 54-week long dispute to a speedy end.

The motion pledging increased support for the strikers was passed unanimously on a show of hands.

Mr Roy Grantham, the secretary of APEX, the clerical union fighting for recognition at Grunwick, said:

of their hearts. They needed sophisticated and detailed plans to bring the firm to heel.

"I shall not disclose the details of our plans," he said. "We do not intend to signal our shots in advance. But action must be positive and effective."

The general council of the TUC had arranged a series of meetings with APEX and other unions which could help, and together they

---

Headline: Cambs Hold-up Drama. Cambridge Evening News

kept asking about the phone. He was looking round all the time. The man was only seconds on the phone. He bought nothing in the cafe and just ran out. He was unshaven and in quite a state. He kept demanding to use the phone. I couldn't hear what he said on the phone, but he was only on it for a few seconds. He just dashed out without saying a word and jumped into a van and drove away. I don't know what kind of van it was.'

Both men were involved in what was to take place soon after on the forecourt of the Autostop Cafe.

Already in the cafe and eating a meal when the second man had gone in and had looked agitatedly around had been two guards from a Security Express van that was on its way from Bedford to an undisclosed destination. It was parked outside. A third guard had stayed with the van and its contents, £200,000 in cash.

The Security Express men, if not regulars, had used the cafe before, perhaps more often than was wise. Gangs of armed robbers would not miss a thing like that. Their movements had probably been monitored over a long time. It must have been known that they would most probably have lunch at the Autostop.

The two guards in the cafe finished their meal and went out, back to their van. As they did so six raiders with sawn-off shotguns roared onto the forecourt in three stolen vehicles, a silver Ford Cortina saloon, making its second visit of the day, a brown Ford Cortina estate and a three ton Ford Trader with a blue cab and a silver body. They had all been stolen in the London area in the previous few days. The gang all wore balaclavas except for one man, wildly brandishing his shotgun, who was wearing a dark blue blazer and had a collar and tie. A smarter kind of armed robber.

One guard managed to get back into the van as a gunman, trying to prevent him closing the door, got his hand trapped in it. Still it was slammed, and two of the guards were out of reach. The gang could only point guns at them through the windows. That had probably not been in their carefully laid and rehearsed plans. In fact, things had probably started to go wrong when the unshaven man in the boiler suit and wellies had got in a state over using the phone. He must have seen that the two security guards were not only in the cafe but had almost finished their meal and would soon be leaving.

The hasty phone call, police believed, had been to a phone box about a mile down the road, where the gang had been waiting. And they had almost been too late. Another couple of seconds and the van would have been back on the road.

As it was, two guards were battened inside it. The raider in the nice, sporty blazer chased the third guard across the forecourt at gunpoint. Tricia Worbey had come out of the cafe at that moment, to get something from a car, and she had seen the attempted hi-jack under way. She said: 'If I had gone outside two minutes earlier I would have been right in the middle of it.' The third security guard, although his own life was being threatened, had been concerned for her life. He had managed to tell her to get back inside the cafe as he was about to be thrown into the back of the Ford Trader. She went on: 'It was then I knew something was going on. But I didn't really know what. I saw a man running round the side of the security van with something in his hand. I couldn't see what it was but I learned later it was a shotgun. I came back inside then.'

Up to that moment, no one in the cafe had had any idea what was going on outside. Peter and Pat Worbey were at work in the back of the building. Their customers were eating, drinking and talking. It was a normal early afternoon. And then the two guards inside the van had activated the internal alarm. A siren had blared out. It was so loud that a bulldozer driver, Andrew Green, at work on a site opposite the cafe, heard it. He said: 'I didn't see anything so I thought it was an electrical fault or something. But then I saw a bloke with his hands in the air and I knew it must be some sort of raid. I started to go across the field.'

The sounding of the siren had alerted the customers in the cafe to the frenzied activity going on outside, and Tricia had gone back in to say what was happening. The raiders knew that someone would be sure to phone the police. There was only one thing that they could do. They had to accept that they had blown it, their attempt to hijack the Security Express van had failed, and all that they could do was make a run for it. And one gang member did just that. In a state of panic he ran away on foot. The rest of the gang made for one of their cars. Andrew Green said: 'The raiders jumped into a brown Ford Cortina and made off. When I spoke to the security men who had been in the van they said that at one stage they turned round to find guns pointing in at them through the back of the van.'

The raiders had pointed their guns but no shots had been fired. Perhaps the only thing that the gang had done right that afternoon. The only injury had been to one of their own men –

a trapped hand. No one and nothing had been hurt – except their own pride in a job well done.

The Cambridgeshire Constabulary immediately put a team of twenty detectives on the case, led by Detective Inspector Pip Grainger under the Cambridge divisional CID commander, Detective Superintendent Keith Hookham.

The gang had left behind the silver Cortina and the Ford Trader as they fled. In the abandoned van police found sticky tape. It was thought that the gang's plan had been to use the tape to bind and gag all the guards inside the Ford van and then to have driven them away to some isolated spot and leave them, locked in. A driver, a swarthy man in a donkey jacket, had been waiting to do that. The other gang members were to have driven the security van away to a pre-arranged safe place where they could all get together and take their time opening the strong boxes before going on their way with £200,000.

The brown Cortina estate, which had probably picked up the athlete en route, had been found abandoned in a lay-by on the A14. The next afternoon Hookham appealed: 'We would like to hear from anyone who saw any of these men or the stolen vehicles before the incident happened. We would especially like to hear from anyone who may have seen the gang switch from the brown Ford estate on a lay-by on the A14. The switch must have occurred around 2-20 to 2-25 and it would have involved six men. This lay-by is about a mile south on the A14 from the A603 junction at New Wimpole.'

That road was already serving the needs of the gangs of silver, art and antiques raiders which for some months had been burgling better-off houses in the area. In November 1976 nearby Wimpole Hall had been robbed. From the point where the brown Cortina had been found, the road could have been used to quickly and easily take the gang anywhere in the country.

Hookham believed that the gang would have split up into two or three cars, which may have been parked in the lay-by for some time. It was vital to get more information. 'The lay-by is on the right hand side going south towards Bassingbourn and we want to hear from anyone who may have seen any cars parked there yesterday afternoon – and, of course, particularly if anyone saw the actual switch take place. Six men would have been involved, so someone must have seen something, however minor they may have thought it was at the time. We want them to please come forward.'

During that interview Keith Hookham had said that the police desperately wanted to hear from anyone who had seen any of the stolen vehicles before the attempted hijack had taken place. Someone had. The Flying Squad. The Sweeney.

Several days before the incident at the Autostop Cafe the Flying Squad had received information from a snout. A brown Ford Cortina estate, registration number UUP 18K, which had recently been stolen in London, was to be used in a robbery. It was to be used either in a bank robbery in south London or in the hijack of a Securicor van in the London area. They were told where it could be found, parked in a north London side-street, and Flying Squad officers did what they had been trained to do – they watched and waited. They went on watching and waiting, but nothing happened. The expected time of the raid came and went, and the car was still there. So the men on obbo made a decision. They would go.

They called their observation off. Regan and Carter would never have done that! They decided that they would hand over to local divisional detectives and they went. But there was a brief gap when no one was watching. By the time the new watchers arrived to continue the surveillance the car was gone. It was on its way to New Wimpole.

No doubt explanations and excuses were trotted out by the Flying Squad officers who had been on duty as to why they had left. There must have been a lot of 'buts' and 'perhaps' being aired.

Perhaps the information that they had been given by the snout had been wrong. They knew their snouts, but, he could have been set up. There was no honour among thieves. Perhaps it had been a deliberate ploy to keep them occupied while some other action was taking place somewhere else. Perhaps the raid had not happened as the snout had told them it would because the gang had got wind of the Sweeney's surveillance on the car. Perhaps it had been a last minute thing to switch targets – from a Securicor van in London to a Security Express van going from Bedford to somewhere and stopping at New Wimpole for lunch. There might even have been – whisper it – a bad squadman somewhere along the line. So close to the edge of the criminal world an officer now and again might go over the edge. In the later 1970s, when the television series was at the height of its popularity, several Flying Squad men ended up banged to rights themselves, jailed for corruption.

Whatever lay behind what the armed robbers and the Flying

Squad had or had not done, one thing about the snout's information had been dead right – the brown Ford Cortina estate had been used.

Whatever the reasoning behind their departure the truth was that if the Flying Squad had stuck to their surveillance for a few more hours and had followed the car out of London and into Cambridgeshire Hookham's interview would have been very different. The gang could have been behind bars and, with them, the agitated tip-off man who had been in too much of a state to say thank you for the use of the phone.

As it was, the armed raiders were free and far away, hoping for better luck next time. They were all back in their own London homes, feet up, watching the telly. Perhaps they were watching *The Sweeney*.

CHAPTER 16

A Clean Kill

1977

I think I have found my happiness and security at last.

At the end of the 1960s, when beautician Maria Tonge was twenty-six and was working in Lincoln, she met firearms expert and keen marksman, John Taylor. He was twenty-eight and her first serious boyfriend. It seemed to both of them to be the ideal relationship. As Maria said: 'We were very fond of each other. I think our love grew.'

After just three months the couple had become engaged. He gave her an engagement ring. An art and antiques lover, as he was, she gave him a painting of the Jew's House in Lincoln to remember the occasion by. She bought and furnished a flat in Lincoln thinking that it would not be too long before they got married, but Taylor wavered over naming the day.

By the end of 1972 she sadly accepted that he probably never would name the day. His intentions, as she told him, were far too casual. She broke off the engagement, sent his ring back to him and moved to Manchester. But, despite all of that, the break between the two of them was far from complete. They exchanged letters, and they still met from time to time.

Maria moved again, that time to Newmarket in Suffolk, about 100 miles from Lincoln, to run her own beautician's business on a top floor of Ashford's department store in the High Street. Then, with experience, she felt confident enough to really strike out on her own and she bought a shop in the town's Old Station Road, close to the heath and the famous Warren Hill gallops and just yards from the Clock Tower at the end of the High Street. There she opened the Maria Tonge Beautique.

Maria Tonge was her business name. She was Barbara Turner, an attractive, petite brunette, always well-groomed and well-dressed. But she preferred to be called Maria. She enjoyed being in Newmarket. She made friends. Her business began to go well. She had her own flat in one of the most select streets in the town, The Avenue, and she felt settled in a place that she liked and amongst people she liked. And perhaps she was happy that, with her move, she had begun to see more of John Taylor again. They got on well and her hopes began to be raised that this time he would feel ready to marry her. But his reluctance to take that next step was still there.

At Christmas 1976, six years after they had first met, she visited him in Lincoln and, while she was there, she asked him straight out whether he ever intended to marry her or not because she was finding the strain too much after so many years. The answer she got from him was an unequivocal 'no'. So, that was that. She went back to Newmarket disillusioned all over again, sure that now their relationship really was over. But neither of them seemed able to make the break final. They

Ashford's Department Store, later Palmer's, Newmarket High Street. The author

Old Station Road towards the Clock Tower and High Street. The author

Old Station Road in 2007. The author

went on meeting.

And then, in September 1977, Maria, at the age of thirty-four, met another man. He was forty-two-year-old Peter Davies, the son of an ex-policeman whose widowed mother lived at New Malden in Surrey. He had had a well-paid job in the machine room of a Fleet Street newspaper but had given that up to find work in Newmarket, drawn there by his love of horseracing. He had become a horsebox driver for trainer Harry Thomson Jones and then he had met Howard Oddy and together they had set up a firm of auctioneers, Mentmore and Grant. Oddy said: 'I introduced him to antiques. He knew nothing about them, but he learned very quickly.' He took to auctioneering and the business built up. After about two and a half years he was ready to buy out his partner. He had bought a cottage in Cheveley, a couple of miles from Newmarket, and he was enjoying renovating it. He was planning to make a future for himself in Newmarket. The only thing that he had lacked had been someone to share that future with. And then he had met Maria Tonge.

He and Maria knew at once that they were meant for each other. After the turbulence and uncertainty of her years with John Taylor the new relationship, after just four or five weeks, seemed to offer all that she could wish for. They were in love and it was taken for granted that they would marry.

But still Maria and Taylor kept in touch, although, now, she really was ready to say her final goodbye. After realising the depth of her feelings for Davies she wrote to Taylor to thank him for the good times that they had known together and telling him of her new love. Her letter had ended with the words: 'I think that at last I have found my true happiness.'

That letter, and especially its ending, brought Taylor to Newmarket to see her. He was very upset. During their meeting he threatened to kill her new lover, but he did sometimes get angry about things and she did not believe him. He was just saying it. In the heat of the moment. He also said that, at last, he was ready to marry her. She had waited so long to hear him say that but, now that the moment had come, it was too late. She was in love with someone else.

Her attachment to Taylor lasted for a few more weeks, into October 1977, and then Maria wrote another letter to him, a letter she may have been wiser not to have written. But then, she had not believed him when he had said that he would kill Davies. What she wrote was: 'After some thought I have finally decided that we should try to make the final break. I think I have found my happiness and security at last.' Those words were to be the propellant to tragedy.

On 24 October, after living with the knowledge for four weeks that he really had lost Maria, Taylor got into his car and again, and for the last time, made that one hundred mile journey to Newmarket, down the A15 and across the fens to visit her. The same journey and the same destination. The difference that day was that with him in the car in a black zip-up bag was a loaded Smith and Wesson revolver and eleven spare rounds of ammunition.

At about four in the afternoon he walked into the Maria Tonge Beautique carrying the black bag. She was surprised to see him. He had not contacted her to say that he was coming. And as soon as she looked at him she was alarmed. She said: 'He had an appearance I had seen before in him. It was a very cold, staring ahead, sort of look. I knew he was in an angry mood.'

It was an anger that might have cost her her life.

He said: 'I have got something to do that I haven't told anybody. I was going to kill you as I came in the door, but after looking at you I couldn't.'

Perhaps Maria did not believe him, as she had not when he had threatened to kill Davies. Or perhaps she thought that his change of mind had defused the situation. A friend popped into the salon for a few minutes and he seemed to calm down. But then, a provocation to an already agitated man, she went into the small kitchen at the back of the shop and began to prepare a meal for the new man in her life.

That roused Taylor again and they were both crying as they went back into the salon. He sobbed: 'There is nothing to live for. I don't care for my firearms or antiques, but he is not going to have you.' At that moment the threat to Maria's life seemed to become real as he unzipped the bag and took out the revolver. But he pointed it at his own head. She said: 'I put my hand over the gun and he told me that it was loaded. He put it down on the couch.'

At that taut, highly-charged moment Peter Davies walked in. The two men in Maria Tonge's life were face to face in the salon amid the perfumes and lotions. The tenseness between the three of them was frightening, reflected in the salon's mirrors.

A conversation began that was to end in death.

Taylor, standing in front of Maria, began it. 'You have taken my girlfriend.'

Davies replied: 'I have done nothing of the sort. I would never take her from you if I believed she was in love with you. I have only heard one side of the story and I believe this has happened before.'

At that point Maria said: 'I had decided to end the relationship for you. Peter has nothing to do with it.'

And then the two men had continued their verbal sparring with Davies saying: 'She is a very nice girl and I think she should be able to make up her own mind.'

Taylor's response was: 'I love her but I haven't had the money to come down and see her.'

'I believe you had money for other things,' Davies said. 'As man to man I think eight years was a long time to keep a girl waiting. You should have known by this time that you love her. You are a sensible man and my first impression of people is not usually wrong. All is fair in love and war.'

Taylor, at that point, had seemed ready to concede that he had lost Maria. He said: 'Well, I had better be going. Will you trust me to be sensible?'

He began to put the gun back into the bag and then, as Maria told the jury at John Taylor's trial at Norwich Crown Court six months later, 'He turned round very sharply and before I had time to think of anything he shot Peter from a range of a few feet. He hit him in the left shoulder. I think there were six shots altogether. The first one I saw. I could not believe it because Peter still stood there. Peter could not believe it either because he reacted in a manner that was shocked and clutched his shoulder. I could not comprehend it because it didn't sound like a revolver. It sounded like a toy pistol.

'The next minute I heard another shot. I put my hands over my eyes. I just screamed and I screamed to hide the gunshots. The third one I thought was for me. I became hysterical and I absolutely bent in half. I thought that one was for me. With total fear, self-preservation came over me. I ran out of the shop and asked people to help and call the police.'

She ran to a neighbouring hairdressing salon. Mrs Vanda Clements said: 'I was in the middle of doing someone'e hair and she came in screaming her head off saying: "Don't let him get me. He will shoot me as well. He has killed Peter. Phone the police or he will kill me."'

Newmarket Journal

Incorporating the Newmarket Free Press, Cambridgeshire and Suffolk General Advertiser.

Thursday, October 27, 1977

No. 4832 Est. 1872

8p

**CHILCOTTS
(NEWMARKET)
LTD.**

TAXIS

Telephone: Newmarket

3282

Firearms researcher in court

MAN CHARGED WITH MURDER

By Maggie Girling

A 36-year-old firearms researcher has been charged with the murder of a Newmarket auctioneer.

Mr John Taylor from Lincoln appeared before a special court in Bury St. Edmunds on Tuesday evening and was remanded in custody until November 3. He did not apply for bail.

The dead man is 42-year-old Mr Peter Davies of Newmarket Road, Cheveley.

● The Maria Tonge beauty salon in Old Station Road, Newmarket.

He was shot at the Maria Tonge beauty salon in Old Station Road, Newmarket at about 4 pm on Monday.

Mr Davies was taken to New Addenbrookes Hospital at Cambridge where a post mortem was carried out on Tuesday morning by Prof. Austin Gresham.

Well known and keenly interested in the racing world, Mr Davies gave up a highly paid job in a Fleet Street machine room when he decided to make his hobby his work.

He came to Newmarket where he worked as a box driver for the trainer, Mr Harry Thomson Jones.

Partner

He established the auctioneer firm of Mentmore and Grant with his partner Mr Howard Oddy about two and half years ago.

"I introduced him to antiques. He knew nothing about them, but he learned very quickly," said Mr Oddy on Tuesday.

"The business had built up well and we were just getting ready for our busy season."

Mr Oddy said that on Friday Mr Davies had agreed to buy his share of the business which would have made Mr Davies the sole owner.

Mr Oddy will concentrate on his interests in ASC Insurance at Wellington Street, Newmarket, where he was partner.

He said Mr Davies was very well-known in the town and made friends with many people.

Mr Oddy said he had known Miss Tonge was Mr Davies' girlfriend. He heard they were going out together about five weeks ago.

Mr Davies was the son of an ex-policeman. His widowed mother lives at New Malden in Surrey where he was brought up.

He was currently modernising his home at Cheveley.

Two youths attacked

Police are investigating an attack on two youths on Newmarket Heath on Tuesday night.

The attack took place at about 11.10 pm on the Heath near London Road.

The youths who were attacked were Alastair Walker of National Stud, Cambridge Road, Newmarket, and Julian Groom of London Road, Newmarket. Both are believed to be in their late teens.

They suffered minor cuts and bruises after they were set upon by four other youths.

Controversy over?

The controversy of the Lark Hill housing development at Moulton seems to be over.

Forest Heath Council has investigated the matter and has sent letters to neighbours saying that there has not been any breach of planning permission.

Headline report from the Newmarket Journal, *25 October 1977.* Newmarket Journal

As grey as death, Maria had then rushed upstairs as Taylor ran past outside the hairdressers.

'About five minutes later she went back to her shop. The man flew after her saying "Don't let her go back in there."'

He knew what she would find.

After the second shot Maria's screams had, for a moment, distracted Taylor. He had turned to her and Davies had seized his chance. He had made for the back door of the salon at the end of a passageway.

Taylor, realising that he had gone, had followed him as Maria had run out into Old Station Road. Following him, he had fired four more shots into Davies' body. He told police later: 'I didn't want to see him suffering. It's all wrong. It's like game. I wanted to make a clean kill. I am wrong. I am wrong. I emptied the gun. It just happened.'

Continuing giving evidence to the jury when Taylor's trial opened at Norwich Crown Court early in May 1978, Maria Tonge said: 'I returned to the shop. Peter was slumped against the back door, blood all over the chest and hands. I saw him dead. I came back into the kitchen. I saw John standing at the desk. He said "I did it for you. I killed him. I loved you."'

The police had arrived quickly after the shooting. The next evening, after Professor Austin Gresham had carried out a post-mortem on the body of Peter Davies at Addenbrooke's Hospital in Cambridge, Taylor appeared before a special court set up in a room at Bury St Edmunds police station. He was remanded in custody to come before Newmarket magistrates on 3 November, charged with murder.

When Taylor's trial opened, Mr Francis Irwin QC, prosecuting said: 'If ever there was an open and shut case of murder this is it. Jealousy is no defence to murder, only a reason. This was a cool, deliberate and calculated murder occasioned by jealousy, and was done as a result of a good deal of thought passing through this man's mind in the previous weeks.'

And yet Taylor, with his ample moustache and eyes blinking behind glasses, appearing in court in a grey business suit and spotted tie, could hardly have looked less like a cold-blooded killer. He pleaded not guilty. And, despite Irwin's accusations of premeditation, even the defendant himself seemed unable to explain what had taken place.

He had turned to leave, as Maria had told the jury. He had said that he was going – and then, 'I am afraid that at that particular moment everything seemed to just disappear. I cannot remember any more at all. I felt something and I was helpless. The next thing I knew some shots had been fired. My first recollection was to feel shock. I was numbed in my mind. I felt it was being done for me. It was very frightening and I can only say the tenseness of the situation culminated where I seemed to lose grip of everything. I cannot explain it. It just seemed suddenly to happen. I was placed in the position where I was responsible for shooting Mr Davies. This was totally against what I was expecting at the time. I am afraid it has left me standing here and I can only express my deepest regret.'

Irwin asked: 'When you fired those shots, for whatever motive, you intended to kill him?'

Taylor replied: 'Yes sir. I cannot recollect the first shot. I did pursue him down the passageway. There was a moment of hesitation. I wanted to put my arm out to support Mr Davies. I turned because Maria screamed. When I turned again I found Mr Davies had disappeared. I fired further shots during that pursuit. I wanted to help the man.'

Overnight, after that first day of the trial, Taylor changed his plea to one of guilty of murder. When the trial resumed at 10-30 the next morning in Court Number 1 it took only two minutes for Judge Griffiths to tell him: 'If it is of any comfort to your peace of mind I should tell you that you made the right decision to change your plea. Because of the evidence you had no defence whatsoever to the charge of murder.'

Maria Tonge, who had been supported by her parents in court on the previous day, was not there to see her ex-fiance led away to begin a life sentence.

Maria Tonge resolutely went back into her closed salon to face the bloodstains on the floor and the bullet holes in the wall. She had received support from the Davies and Taylor families as well as from her own, but she was still shattered, on tranquillisers and finding sleep illusory. The tragedy cost her her health, her happiness, her business and her savings.

She was determined to stay on in Newmarket where everyone had been so kind and caring to her. She would find a job and start a fresh life. She refused offers of large sums of money to sell her story to one or other of the national newspapers, feeling that all three families involved needed to put the past behind them and to have their privacy restored.

But she did give a lengthy interview to the local paper, the

Newmarket Journal. A thank you to the town where she felt she belonged.

Throughout her ordeal, Maria had been comforted and bolstered by her Roman Catholic faith. It had given her an inner strength, and it would continue to do so. Immediately after the trial she went to a convent in the Suffolk countryside for a few weeks retreat from all that had taken place. She returned to Newmarket hopeful that she would be able to build that new life for herself, would be able to enjoy new friendships and would be able to be the woman she had been before the shooting – but it did not work.

Peter Davies, she knew, would have told her that life must go on. It did. But not as it had been before, when they had both looked forward to a shared future. She went back to the convent, and stayed.

CHAPTER 17

The A1 Murder

1983

Millions of television viewers saw a ten minute reconstruction . . .

About nine o'clock on the morning of Sunday 11 September 1983, David Hurst, a banker from Northwood in Middlesex, was taking part in a twelve hour cycle time trial along the A1. He stopped at a lay-by between Brampton and Buckden, near Huntingdon. He had arranged to meet his wife and son there for a break, for some food and a hot drink. After his refreshments, he decided to take the opportunity to relieve himself before going on his way. There was a roadside hedge. That would do. He could go behind that. But he would have to cross a ditch to reach it.

It was as he did so that he saw the body of a woman lying in the bottom of the ditch. He later said: 'I could see the whole of it. There had been no attempt to hide it and whoever did it didn't seem to have tried to move it. That was something that surprised me. It was quite clean, but when you looked at the head there was no mistake that she was dead.'

The woman was lying face down in the ditch and she had been severely battered about the head. The family drove to the Brampton Hut Motel, about a mile away, and the police were called from there.

From the start, the Cambridgeshire police had a puzzle to solve. Who was she? It was essential to know her identity for their enquiries to proceed, but there was not a scrap of identification on the body or to be found anywhere around it. The area was searched but no weapon was found and there were no signs that a struggle had taken place, although it was considered likely that she had been killed at or close to the lay-by within the past twenty-four hours. Fragments of bone and flesh were found near to the body.

Detective Chief Superintendent Len Bradley, the head of the Cambridgeshire CID, assumed responsibility for the murder investigation. With nothing to identify her, one of his first actions was to issue a description of the dead woman. It was the most obvious way to go ahead. And someone, somewhere, must have known her.

She was aged between twenty-five and thirty-five and was of slight build. She had grey-green eyes and dark brown hair, just above collar length. She was wearing a thick, white Arran-style sweater, blue jeans and lace-up blue or black white-soled canvas shoes. She had a gold wedding ring and she was still wearing her gold Omega wristwatch.

A closer examination was made and a post-mortem was carried out by Dr Ian Hill at Peterborough District Hospital. Dr Hill found horrific injuries. The dead woman had multiple fractures – to her skull, her nose, her jaw and a wrist – and she had cuts and bruises over most parts of her body. The fracture to the wrist had probably been received as she had tried to defend herself from her attacker. There was no doubt that she had put up a fight. She had not gone quietly. The injuries, Dr Hill believed, had been caused by a blunt instrument wielded with considerable force. So much force had been used that part of her skull had been almost sheared off. Death, unsurprisingly, had been due to cerebral haemorrhage and a fractured skull.

Dr Hill also reported that she had eaten and had drunk alcohol two to three hours before her death. She had eaten a light meal of tomatoes and grapes, and perhaps oranges. All of her teeth had been capped, one of them with gold, and she had a distinctive mole on the thigh of her left leg. Dr Hill also found traces of sand on her feet. She had a suntan and from that it could be seen that she had been wearing a swimsuit.

Checks began on local restaurants where she may have eaten that last meal, and details of her dental work and of her gold, bracelet-style watch were publicised. Drawings were made of the watch, which was not one to go unnoticed on the wrist of a friend or relative, and they appeared in the press along with copies of markings found on it.

It was likely that the woman had been comfortably off, if not wealthy. Her dental work was expensive, as was her rectangular watch, made in 1969. It had jeweller's repair marks on the back which police hoped would be recognised by someone.

Her sweater was far from cheap too. It was a Woolgatherers Original with a sheep and lambs motif. Her sweater, jeans and, most of all, her canvas shoes, caused detectives to wonder if she had been dressed for sailing. They were hopeful. Enquiries were made amongst the sailing crowd at nearby Grafham Water, but no one there knew her. A blank.

The police went public. They made a direct appeal for information and in the first two days of the investigation they had 'a terrific response', but nothing definite was forthcoming. No one had seen two people, perhaps arguing or struggling, at the lay-by on the A1. No one had seen a woman answering the description they had circulated. She still had no identity and no name.

By Tuesday 13 September Bradley was desperate to have that identification made. In an interview he said: 'Surely someone must know this woman from the detailed description we have already issued.'

He would not have much longer to wait before someone did. It was the coming-together of the various concerned people in the life of thirty-six-year-old London solicitor, Mrs Janice Weston, that brought it about. An anxious Anthony Weston, her thirty-nine-year-old husband, a property developer and financial advisor, had been on a business trip to France. On his return, he could not locate his wife. At the same time, Mrs Weston's fellow partners in the London law firm of Charles Russell and Co in Lincoln's Inn were equally anxious. She had failed to arrive for work on the Monday morning and they had not been able to contact her at her flat in Holland Park.

And then had come about the increasingly fearful exchange of concerns between Janice Weston's fellow solicitors and her family. A foreboding had gripped them as they had acknowledged that the details of an unknown murdered woman, issued by police and spread across the newspapers, fitted her exactly.

It was delegated to her brother-in-law to call the police and give the body a name at last. A colleague from the law firm volunteered to see the body for identification and confirmed their fears. But, by then, it was expected. It was Janice. Anthony Weston, Janice's husband of fifteen months, was being comforted by friends.

At last the bludgeoned body had become a person, with a past if not a future. The police knew who and what the woman in the ditch had been and they could begin to put together a picture of her life and, hopefully, discover what had brought her to that lay-by on the A1 and her appointment with death.

Janice Weston, who had continued to work under her maiden name of Wright, was a convent-educated woman who had been born in Bromley in Kent but had been raised in Potter's Bar, on the outskirts of London. She had studied law at Manchester

Universityy, where she had gained a First, and then, after twelve years with another law firm, she had joined Charles Russell and Company in August 1981. In February 1982 she had become one of fourteen partners in the firm.

She was a high-flier who specialised in international finance and conveyancing, handling multi-million pound property deals for international companies. She was also an expert in the field of computer fraud, a relatively new concept in the early 1980s, and she had been working on a book on data protection.

An attractive, vibrant woman, she had had many friends and a good social life. On 2 September, just nine days before her murder, she had returned from a holiday in France with her husband and two friends. She had been worthy of respect in her professional life and she had been good at her job. In all, she had been well liked by everyone and she had had the proverbial 'not an enemy in the world'.

The discovery of her handbag still at her flat, although with no purse in it, was considered significant by police. As Bradley said: 'She was a happily married, happy-go-lucky girl. A woman like that doesn't go far without her handbag.'

But she had.

The most important information to come from Janice Weston's identification, something hopefully to take the investigation further, was about the car that she had been driving. It had been a silver Alfa Romeo Alfetta saloon with a roof rack.

Almost as soon as its details and licence number were publicised in the press and on television Huntingdon police received a phone call from a member of the public. Little over an hour later, by 10 pm on the Wednesday evening, the police had followed up that call and were in the Regent's Park area of north-west London. They were quickly able to confirm that the car which had been reported as having been there since Monday was the one that they were looking for. It was Janice's car. It was covered and put on a trailer and taken back to Huntingdon for examination by forensic experts.

They found blood. It was unmistakable. It was everywhere. Most of it was on the driver's side of the car. Blood was on the steering wheel, the controls, the transmission tunnel, the door and the windscreen. A bloodstained tissue, or something of that kind, had probably been used to wipe the windscreen to allow whoever had been at the wheel a view of the road ahead when it had been driven after the murder. Bloodstains on the door indicated that Mrs Weston had been attacked while she had been in or near the car. It was most probable that she had been assaulted near the driver's seat and with the door of the car open.

Forensic scientist, John Hayward, thought that Mrs Weston had, at some point, been taken from the car and there had been a 'violent and sustained attack with a heavy weapon while she lay in the ditch'.

There was little doubt that whoever had wiped the windscreen and had driven the Alfa Romeo from the Cambridgeshire lay-by into London, would have been extremely bloodstained. Bradley was hopeful. 'There must have been a great deal of blood. I would have thought that the killer, having got out of the car, some person – perhaps a brother, father or wife – would know that this person had been involved in something serious.'

Perhaps they had, but no one came forward to say so.

Mrs Weston's purse had not been in the car when it had been recovered. Also missing from it had been the spare wheel, the wheel brace and its Alfa Romeo snake and sword grille badge. A gruesome souvenir?

Still missing, too, were nine hours in Mrs Weston's life. Her last hours.

The hours immediately before those hours could partly be pieced together. At 11-20 on the morning of Saturday 10 September she had picked up a wheel from a London garage. She had then gone to her office in Lincoln's Inn. She was said by one of her colleagues to have been 'perfectly normal and relaxed', but another had seen her look from the office window on several occasions, as if she had been expecting someone to be there, waiting for her. She had left her office at 4-15 pm.

And that had been it. From then on there had been no sightings of her, no indication of where she might have gone and why and whether she had been alone. She had gone, and by midnight she had been dead. Those intervening, unaccounted-for hours were a complete blank. All that the police could do at that stage was to fill them with guesses and suppositions.

She may have been on her way to Clopton Manor, a property owned by Mrs Weston and her husband, which was about fourteen miles ahead of the lay-by along the A1. She may have stopped to change a wheel in the lay-by, but the tools to do that, and the spare wheel, had not been in the car. She may have known her killer. She may not have known her killer. She may have stopped to pick up a hitchhiker. Her husband said that at one time she would have done so, but he knew that she had not done so recently. It was not safe. So many ifs and maybes.

Meanwhile, the thorough, routine police work went on. In just a few weeks 5,000 people would be interviewed and 12,000 pages of statements would be taken. All police leave was cancelled and officers were drafted in from other areas. With Mrs Weston living and working in London, and her car having been found there, the Metropolitan Police also became involved.

On Thursday 15 September, five days after the body had been found, the police staged a dramatic reconstruction with Huntingdon policewoman, WPC Penny Aldred, dressed as Janice Weston filmed and photographed at the lay-by. Road checks were set up, motorists were flagged down and regular users of the A1 were asked if they had seen the Alfa Romeo at that spot. The car had been brought to the lay-by and was illuminated with floodlights. It was a busy road, but no one had seen the Alfa Romeo, or Mrs Weston, or a struggle between two people.

From the lay-by, the car was taken back to the London street where it had been abandoned and a similar exercise was carried out. Several people came forward there to say that they remembered seeing the car parked there on the Monday, Tuesday and Wednesday, up to the time when the police had been told of its location, but no one had seen the driver. Blood-covered, as police said that the person would be, they would have remembered if they had.

On 20 September, ten days after the murder, an inquest into Mrs Weston's death was opened and adjourned, the first of four adjournments that would take the police investigation into the spring of 1984. On each occasion Mrs Weston's husband and her family asked for her body to be released for cremation. On each occasion they were refused. It could not be released until it became certain that a second post-mortem would not be necessary.

Despite the thoroughness of the investigation by more than one police force there seemed to be a puzzling lack of progress. They seemed – perhaps 'clueless' was an appropriate word to describe the apparent stalemate. And then, in December, three months after Janice Weston's murder, her husband was taken into custody. Anthony Weston spent fifty-three hours in police custody being questioned about his wife's death. He was then released on police bail until February while a report on the case was prepared and considered by the Director of Public

Prosecutions. February came without the DPP having reached a decision, so Weston's bail was extended.

During that time, in January, when Mrs Weston's will was published, it was found that she had left £414,000, a sum bolstered by the almost £150,000 an elderly tycoon, Heinz Eisner, head of the Mettoy company, had bequeathed to her in 1977. Her husband was not left a lump sum in her will, but he was to receive around £200,000 of the residue for life. The money was to be available to him while he was alive, but it was to go back to the estate when he died.

At about the same time, Clopton Manor was put up for sale, with the east wing on the market for £77,000.

It was Friday 30 March before Bradley was able to clear up the situation regarding Weston. In a statement he said: 'Following consultations with the DPP, no criminal proceedings are being instituted against Mr Anthony Weston. He has been released from his bail recognisance to attend Huntingdon Police Station on Monday.'

Bradley went on to say that, after almost seven months of extensive investigation and although the file on the murder was still to be kept open, positive lines of enquiry were dwindling. The size of the police operation was, therefore, going to be reduced. The police still lacked that vital piece of information that would lead to an arrest.

The final inquest into the murder of Janice Weston was held in Huntingdon in mid-April 1984. It took the jury only a few minutes to return their verdict of unlawful killing. Both the deputy coroner, Paul Rogers, and Bradley, stressed after the hearing that information on the killing was still being sought.

That is still the case.

On Monday 1 October 1984, just over a year after her murder, the BBC programme *Crimewatch UK* featured the unsolved killing of Janice Weston. Millions of television viewers saw a ten minute reconstruction of Mrs Weston's actual and probable movements on the day of her death, in London and at the A1 lay-by where her killer had struck. She was seen collecting a spare wheel from the London garage, shopping and working in her office, before driving to her death.

More than 120 calls were taken at the BBC's Lime Grove studios and by police in Peterborough. Detective Chief Superintendent Len Bradley appeared on television, discussing some of the calls in the studio with the programme's co-presenter, Sue Cook. Most significantly, one viewer had called the BBC claiming that he had changed a wheel on the Alfa Romeo on the night that Janice Weston was murdered, a call that Bradley said was 'remarkable'. The call would be checked out at once.

Five callers reported having seen Mrs Weston with her car in the lay-by, and another thought that he had seen a man in a shop in Royston, only hours after the body had been found, buying duplicate number plates for her car.

But most of the calls related to sightings of a wheel, lying about somewhere, which numerous informants thought may be the one still missing from the Alfa Romeo. A lot of checking had to be done of a lot of wheels. And none of them turned out to be the one being sought.

Although the programme's co-presenter, Nick Ross, told viewers that the feedback on that particular case had been below average, a police spokesman said: 'I think there is a distinct possibility this has taken the inquiry further.'

The most crucial information was that coming from the man who had called and had said that he had changed the wheel of the Alfa Romeo in the lay-by. As Bradley said, it had immediately been followed up. But the call soon became just one more baffling unknown in a baffling murder case.

Chief Inspector Kevin Phillip said the next day: 'The man who claims to have changed the wheel has not been traced and his claim has not yet been substantiated.' He had not been found at the address he had given. He has still not been found.

The *Crimewatch* reconstruction had left the inquiry more or less where it had been before, and where it had been for the past year. As the police put it, 'No significant progress has been made so far.'

In September 2006, twenty-three years after the bloody murder of Janice Weston, a BBC spokesperson confirmed that there has been no one arrested and no one charged in relation to it.

That vital piece of information is still awaited.

CHAPTER 18

Mind the Baby?

1984–86

Now it's murder!

It was raining heavily. The lights of the small village shop and post office lanced out over the gleaming pavement and into the road in the early evening darkness. The shop door was open although it was six o'clock, past the usual closing time. It should have been locked up with the lights out.

At six o'clock a neighbour, Colin Tibbs, left his home nearby and walked to his car. As he did so, he heard groaning noises. Later he said: 'I thought it was children messing about in the village hall, but as I drove past the post office I saw that the lights were on, the door was open, and Doreen lying there covered in blood.'

In the Cambridgeshire village of Thriplow, eight or nine miles to the south of Cambridge, the postmistress, Doreen Smith, a widow in her early fifties, had been gunned down, shot in the head at close range, as she had been about to close at 5-30 on Friday 5 October 1984 and had been counting the day's takings.

Led by George Sutherland, forty Cambridge-based police officers were brought in and enquiries began. An incident room was set up at their Parkside headquarters as they went house-to-house in Thriplow and leafleted surrounding villages. The village hall, opposite the post office, was used for taking hundreds of statements from the 600 or so villagers and from the shop's customers.

Many of the customers stopped to use the shop as they were passing through the village. Although not a main route the road outside the shop connected to other villages in the area, and Cambridge, Royston and Saffron Walden could be reached. It was handy for many people, especially going to and from work, as Sutherland found. He said: 'It has now been established that considerable numbers of people travel through the village to and from their place of work and home and use the shop to obtain bits and pieces of shopping. They normally call after 5 pm at night.'

The Post Office immediately offered a £5,000 reward for information. It took the attack very seriously. Post offices, especially in the villages, were considered vital for pensioners, young mothers and anyone unable to get far from home easily, and people were always needed to run them. It was not an attractive job. Raids and break-ins happened too often. They could be seen as an easy target and the prospect of becoming the victim of such a crime was off-putting. It had to be seen to care very much about what had happened to Doreen Smith. It delivered the police leaflets free of charge.

The day after the robbery, Sutherland said that Mrs Smith had been shot once in the head with a small calibre weapon and that robbery had been the motive. The last customer to have seen her alive had called at the shop at 5-25 pm and she had been cashing up the post office.

As he spoke, Mrs Smith lay in the Intensive Care Unit of Addenbrooke's Hospital in Cambridge. She was on life support, having undergone an emergency operation. There was still a bullet lodged in her brain. She was, as was usually said in such circumstances, 'fighting for her life'.

It was likely that that last customer had left the shop just a few minutes before the gunman had walked in and robbed her of what was thought to have been just a little over £400. Sutherland said: 'For such a small sum it's difficult to understand why such an inordinate amount of violence was necessary to overcome Mrs Smith, who was alone at the time.'

New Addenbrooke's Hospital, Hills Road, where Mrs Smith died.
Cambridgeshire Collection

In the next few days, little headway was made. Despite intensive police work they had no description of any likely suspect and no one had 'coppered', although Sutherland thought that the attacker was probably local or, at least, had been known to the victim. He was sure that the gunman lived 'nearer rather than distant'.

Then things moved on a little bit. A week after the shooting it was revealed in the local press that the police wanted to speak to three men who had visited two country sports shops in Newmarket on the afternoon of the raid trying to buy .22 ammunition, the calibre used to shoot Mrs Smith. On each occasion, one man had entered the shop while two had stayed outside in a small, off-white saloon car, a Morris or an Austin 1100. It was the first of several red herrings that would take valuable police time but, of course, that was not known at the time and the information had to be followed up.

On Tuesday 23 October, eighteen days after the raid, Doreen Smith lost that fight for her life. After her death in Addenbrooke's, Sutherland, somewhat obviously, said: 'Now it's murder!' Perhaps it was the voicing of a new vital purpose given to his officers, now increased to sixty, who were working on the case. There was the killer of an innocent woman to be caught. He went on to say of his men: 'It has saddened the officers investigating the crime but strengthened their resolve and deter-mination in their hunt for the killers.' He had decided that two men had been responsible, and he ended by appealing for anyone with any information about them to come forward. Information or not, no one did so.

On the same day, it was announced that the police now had not one, but four, leads. They were the men, now reduced to two, who had tried to buy ammunition in Newmarket, and three vehicles which had been seen in the vicinity of the post office some time after 5-30 on the day in question. The Post Office had delivered leaflets about several cars the police wished to 'eliminate from their enquiries' and they had been reduced to three. The vehicles were an off-white, medium saloon, a large, brown, four-door saloon, and an old Volkswagen caravanette, maroon with a white roof and foreign number plates.

The saloons had been seen at 5-40 and about 5-50. Who had been driving them? And the clapped-out caravanette? That had been seen parked on a farm track near the post office at the time of the raid. An unlikely robbery or getaway vehicle but – it had to be checked. Two officers were given the task of tracking it down. They scoured the surrounding villages. It was a matter of foot-slogging. Good old police work. And they found it. It was in the village of Stapleford, about halfway between Thriplow and Cambridge.

They were soon knocking on the door of a house in Stapleford. The woman who owned the house knew almost

Stapleford Village sign. The author

nothing about either the caravanette or its driver, but she knew someone who did know both – her daughter, Maureen Cottage. At that point, an end was put to Sutherland's 'nearer rather than distant' idea. The man that the police were seeking was a Greek petty criminal called George Farmakopoulos.

It would take ten months, the Cambridgeshire police, Interpol and the police forces of three European countries, to bring Farmakopoulos back to Cambridge and justice, and it may not have been brought about at all without the troubled conscience and remorse of Maureen Cottage.

Farmakopoulos, in his thirties, was a nomad, a continental wanderer of no fixed abode, who had roamed throughout Europe for a decade or more, picking up foreign languages if nothing more. He had lived by his wits. Small crimes and begging had given him a scant, hand-to-mouth existence which had often brought him to the notice of the police. He was known to Interpol under a variety of names, but to the police of his native country, Greece, he was known by his birth name of Farmakopoulos. His offences ranged from theft to vagrancy to criminal damage, and he had served several prison sentences,

Stapleford village scene. The author

but for nothing anywhere near the seriousness of armed robbery. During one of those sentences the journey that would take him into Maureen's life and to that rainy village in Cambridgeshire had begun.

In a Zurich prison Farmakopoulos had met Maureen's husband, Michael, imprisoned for drug smuggling. He had given Farmakopoulos Maureen's Amsterdam address and, on his release, he had wasted no time in getting in touch.

Maureen, also in her thirties and the mother of a baby boy, was known on the Amsterdam drug scene through her husband and his connections, and also as a user. She was someone who was on the edge of what action there was, a fringe associate of those who were criminally involved.

When Farmakopoulos turned up on her doorstep she was charmed by the bearded Greek who knew how to flatter. He considered himself something of a ladies' man and trotted out stories of a moneyed lifestyle that were rather at odds with the indigent reality. A relationship had begun. It was to end with Doreen Smith's murder.

In Munich, Farmakopoulos had bought the Volkswagen caravanette and it had opened up new travel possibilities for both of them. They decided that they would visit Maureen's mother in Stapleford. It would be an opportunity for her to see something of her small grandson and to get to know the new, charismatic man in her daughter's life. That was the idea. But her mother, older and perhaps less easily impressed upon, was not as enamoured as Maureen. She did not take to Farmakopoulos and he was made to sleep in the caravanette outside her home. While there, Maureen realised that she could be pregnant with Farmakopoulos' baby and for that reason, and the coolness of their reception, they decided that they would go back to Amsterdam. Her pregnancy could be confirmed at her doctor's there.

Farmakopoulos was still regaling everyone he met with his tall tales, his fantasy world, of fast cars, faster women, and the enviable health of his finances. He was loaded. He told Maureen and her mother of his wealth, of the land and property he owned in the United States, and, to add a little local colour, of his own plane which he piloted himself and kept at Marshall's airfield in Cambridge. All of that could hardly have been further from the reality of his life as a penurious drifter with his knackered caravanette which only got going, with a bit of luck, if it was push-started. He had no money at all and that was

Small private aircraft at Marshall's Airport, Cambridge. The author

definitely not part of being the man that he claimed to be.

In Stapleford his lack of money really got to him. He had to have money. It became an obsession. There must be a way, somehow, to get money. He gave it a lot of thought, and then he knew what he would do. He would rob a post office in one of the little villages around Stapleford. It would be a doddle. He would have the money he needed and they would be back on the continent and in the clear quick as a wink. Easy.

For more than two weeks he talked of his plan. He went on and on about finding some small, isolated post office and

Stapleford village centre from the Cambridge-Thriplow road. The author

robbing it. Then he made his choice. It would be Thriplow post office. Maureen, from the start, did not like the idea, but she was in his thrall, completely dominated, and he wore her down. At last, she agreed to go along.

A wet, gloomy Friday afternoon seemed perfect. It would be even easier in the rain with fewer people about, fewer customers. They set off after lunch and called to see some friends where they left Maureen's son. The friends said that they would be pleased to babysit until they called back. They would not be very long. They carried on to Thriplow.

The rain had brought an early darkness. Farmakopoulos parked where he could watch the lighted post office and the comings and goings of the shop' customers. It was a popular shop and its owner was a well liked, happy woman who had taken the business over two years before, after the death of her husband, Richard.

The last customer had left, the last of her life. She was in the post office and had begun to get ready to close. Farmakopoulos and Maureen went into the shop together. Maureen had been told that she was to distract the postmistress. She had hardly had time to start doing that when Farmakopoulos had appeared behind the post office counter and told Doreen Smith to put the money that she was counting into a paper bag. He held a gun in both hands and it was pointed at the woman's head.

Maureen had known that Farmakopoulos had a gun. It was kept in the caravanette, wrapped in a tea towel. But she had not known that he had intended to take it into the post office with him. She had stepped back from the post office then, into the shop, startled by the gun but not believing for a moment that he intended to use it. It must just be to scare the woman.

She said, much later, that she did not hear or see Farmakopoulos shoot, although she had heard the woman cry: 'No, don't!'

Farmakopoulos left with £415-2s in his paper bag. £200 in the shop till was left behind. They had to push-start the caravanette to get away.

It had been on the way back to pick up Maureen's son and go on home to Stapleford for tea that Farmakopoulos had told Maureen that he had forced the postmistress into a cupboard in her living quarters and had shot her four times.

The next day, they left Cambridge and England, after Farmakopoulos had given the caravanette to a friend in Stapleford, telling him not to take it out on the road but to use it for spare motor parts.

Cambridge police now knew the man they wanted to question regarding the Thriplow shooting. The next stage was to catch him and bring him back to Parkside. It was not to be easy. Interpol, the international police network, was alerted as Farmakopoulos and Maureen made the long journey from Calais to Antwerp and then on to Amsterdam, where Maureen's pregnancy was confirmed.

Constantly on the move, they then went back to Antwerp. After that, they went on to Munich and then to Athens.

In Amsterdam they had read about their raid on the post office, of Doreen Smith dragging herself across the shop floor to the door, of her battle to stay alive, and, finally, of her losing that battle after eighteen days. George Farmakopoulos had become a wanted man, a murderer.

Appalled at the outcome of their robbery Maureen wanted to go back to England and give herself up to the police. It was something that she felt she had to do. It was the only way that she would be able to live with herself.

Farmakopoulos was made of harder stuff. There would be no

Entrance to Parkside, Cambridgeshire Constabulary headquarters. The author

going back for either of them. He took Maureen's passport and forced her to go on with him, going from one European city to another. But she was still determined that she must face the consequences of that October afternoon in Thriplow, so much so that, when they returned to live in Athens, Farmakopoulos locked her in the house.

She was, however, in contact with her mother who sent her money. She had had none of her own. She took an opportunity to search the house and, when she found her passport, she managed to escape and make for the airport where she took a flight to Heathrow and into the waiting arms of the Cambridge police. The crime which, up to that point, had been something of a first-timer for the local force, something they could never have had to deal with before, became, with Maureen Cottage's compliance, an example of British and European policing at its most ingenious.

Maureen had been arrested as she landed at Heathrow airport on Sunday 6 January 1985. From there she had been taken straight to Parkside police station in Cambridge and had been charged with the murder of Doreen Smith. On the Tuesday, she was hustled into the Cambridge magistrate's court under a blanket to be remanded in custody.

She had returned voluntarily to face the consequences of the Thriplow robbery and murder and she made it known that she was willing to help the police in any way that she could to have Farmakopoulos caught. It was known from the outset that it would take deception and lies to lure him from his Athens hideaway. And they had already begun. He had no idea that she had been arrested on her return to Cambridge. He believed that Maureen had run away to the arms of her mother, not those of the police. He thought that she was at home in Stapleford where she would stay for the birth of her baby. They would be reunited after the birth the happy little family.

In all, Farmakopoulos was to be bamboozled for eight months, during which time Maureen gave birth to his daughter – in prison. Months in which the whole thing needed careful and constant organisation because, naturally, he wanted to be in contact with his lover. Problems were tackled with military precision. When he phoned her Stapleford home, where he believed her to be, Maureen's mother had to use delaying tactics. She could say anything, make any excuse, just keep him dangling, while Maureen was whisked from her prison cell to her home to make or take a call.

Behind it all, the purpose, was the arrest of Farmakopoulos. He had remained hidden. He had to be enticed into the open. It was decided that Maureen would tell him that the time had come for that reunion they both wanted so desperately. It was set up. Maureen told him that she and her new baby daughter – his daughter – would travel to Amsterdam and meet him there. He was told which hotel she would be staying in. The hotel was told to expect a phone call from Farmakopoulos. With Maureen still in prison in England, he was to be drawn to Amsterdam where the Dutch police would be waiting to welcome him.

But Farmakopoulos had lived on his wits from his teens. He had the wariness of a street animal. He agreed to go to Amsterdam, but he did not trust airports. He would certainly not fly there. He would take the train. He did – but to Paris. When he got to Paris he had another long think about Amsterdam. He was not happy about Amsterdam. There was something in the air? Was it a smell? One that was decidedly fishy? He felt so.

From Paris he phoned Maureen at her Amsterdam hotel, only, of course, she was still in her prison cell in England. The primed hotel staff told him that she could not come to the phone straight away because she was feeding the baby. She would call him back as soon as she could. When the message was relayed by the Dutch police, and she did call him back, all the carefully laid police entrapments were instantly upturned. His instinctive, self-preservation had kicked in, and Amsterdam was out. He had said that he would meet her the next day, as arranged, but it would be in Antwerp.

The intricate police operation was quickly switched from Holland to Belgium and a new set of police officers was put on alert. Again he would use the train to take him to that reunion with Maureen and a first glimpse of his baby daughter. He liked trains. He trusted trains.

As he left the train in Antwerp, he was arrested.

He did not come without a struggle. In prison in Antwerp he fought extradition to Britain for questioning by Cambridge detectives with appeal after appeal. It was August 1985 before, finally, charged with the murder of Doreen Smith, he was flown to Heathrow, accompanied on the flight by Cambridge police officers.

In February 1986, Farmakopoulos and Maureen Cottage came up for trial before Mr Justice Farqharson at Norwich Crown Court. Farmakopoulos may have been, or may have considered himself to be, a ladies man, but he was no constant lover.

When the murder charge against Maureen was dropped leaving only a charge of robbery to be considered by the jury, Farmakopoulos did his best to put all the blame onto her. Through his defence, Bruce Laughland QC, he accused her of lying to save her own skin and to protect her real accomplices in the Thriplow shooting. He claimed that she had struck a deal with the police to have the murder charge against herself dropped and Farmakopoulos, who had not been with her on the raid but had been shopping in Cambridge at the time, blamed for it to protect her real partners in the crime.

Laughland attacked her. 'You want to conceal the identity of your true accomplice or accomplices, people of whom you may be in fear or for whom you may have some regard. He or they were persons derived from your long association with criminals involved with drugs or violence.' She was made to suffer a bombardment of high-pressure accusations, including that she carried firearms, and her integrity, her honesty and her lifestyle were shot to pieces.

She agreed that she had lived in the criminal drugs underworld of Amsterdam for several years before she had met Farmakopoulos and had used cannabis, cocaine and heroin. But she denied his allegations about the shooting, calling them complete fiction, like the fantasy world he lived in, and saying that he had been the driving force behind the Thriplow robbery and murder and that he had been the one who had carried them out.

As the jury was about to retire to consider its verdict at the end of the trial, workmen accidentally cut off the electricity supply. The court was plunged into an eery darkness. The jury's six and a half hours of deliberations were carried out by gaslight before their verdict was returned.

Farmakopoulos was found guilty of murder by a majority of eleven to one. He was sentenced to life imprisonment. Maureen Cottage got five years imprisonment for her part in the robbery.

Farmakopoulos went berserk in court, lunging at police officers and screaming at them that they were liars. There was a violent struggle before he could be hustled out of court and down to the cells while his many Greek relatives, over in Norwich for the trial, screamed abuse from the public gallery.

Farqharson told Sutherland: 'The skill with which this inquiry was conducted reflects greatly upon you and your colleagues.' The colleagues of the Cambridge force had been spread across Europe, in Athens, Amsterdam and Antwerp, distant rather than near, as Farmakopoulos himself had turned out to be.

Maureen resolved to put her life in order and to make a fresh start, for herself and for her children. Once she was at liberty again, she would do just that.

Select Bibliography

Books and Journals

Camps, Francis E, *Camps on Crime*, David and Charles, Newton Abbot, 1973

Church, Robert, *Murder in East Anglia*, Robert Hale, London, 1987

Close, David H, *Greece Since 1945*, Pearson Education, Harlow, 2002

Danson, Cyril 'The Cambridge Rapist', *True Detective*, April 1980, 4-14 and 50

Hotson, Bernard E 'The Cambridge Riot: February 13th, 1970,' *The Police Journal*, volume 44, no 1, January-March 1971, 61-68

Kirby, Dick *The Real Sweeney Robinson*, London, 2005

Lane, Brian, *The Encyclopaedia of Forensic Science*, Headline, London, 1992

Mason, Gary, *The Official History of the Metropolitan Police*, Carlton, London, 2004

Ruff's Guide to the Turf 1976, Sporting Life, London, 1976

Thurlow, David *Evil in East Anglia*, Robert Hale, London, 1993

Newspapers

Cambridge Daily News
Cambridge Evening News
Cambridge Independent Press
Hunts Post
Newmarket Journal
Royston Crow
The Times

TRUE CRIME FROM WHARNCLIFFE

Foul Deeds and Suspicious Deaths Series

Staffordshire and The Potteries
Colchester
Manchester
Guilford
Derby
Northampton
Pontefract and Castleford
Tees
Bedford
Bristol
Carlisle
Newcastle
Southend-on-Sea
Barnsley
Birmingham
Blackburn and Hyndburn
Chesterfield
Coventry
Ealing
Guernsey
Huddersfield
Leeds
Liverpool
Newport
Nottingham
Rotherham
London's East End
Wigan

More Foul Deeds Wakefield
Mansfield
Leicester
Stratford and South Warwickshire
Brighton
Folkestone and Dover
Oxfordshire
Black Country
Durham
Bradford
Cambridge
Halifax
Scunthorpe
Barking, Dagenham & Chadwell Heath
Bath
More Foul Deeds Birmingham
Bolton
More Foul Deeds Chesterfield
Croydon
Grimsby
Hampstead, Holborn and St Pancras
Hull
Lewisham and Deptford
London's West End
Norfolk
Portsmouth
Warwickshire
York

OTHER TRUE CRIME BOOKS FROM WHARNCLIFFE

Norfolk Mayhem and Murder
The A-Z of London Murders
Unsolved Murders in Victorian and
    Edwardian London
Unsolved Yorkshire Murders
A-Z Yorkshire Murder
Brighton Crime and Vice 1800-2000
Essex Murders

Executions & Hangings in Newcastle
    and Morpeth
Norwich Murders
Unsolved Norfolk Murders
Yorkshire's Murderous Women
Black Barnsley
Durham Executions
Strangeways Hanged

Please contact us via any of the methods below for more information
or a catalogue.

WHARNCLIFFE BOOKS
47 Church Street – Barnsley – South Yorkshire – S70 2AS
Tel: 01226 734555 – 734222 Fax: 01226 – 734438
E-mail: enquiries@pen-and-sword.co.uk
Website: www.wharncliffebooks.co.uk

Index